MR. CHEAP

GUIDE TO PAYING FOR COLLEGE

Go to School Without Going Broke

B.A. CHEAP
Technical Review by Sheryle Proper

adamsmedia
avon, massachusetts

Copyright © 2008 by F+W Publications, Inc. All rights reserved.
This book, or parts thereof, may not be reproduced in any
form without permission from the publisher; exceptions are
made for brief excerpts used in published reviews.

Published by
Adams Media, an F+W Publications Company
57 Littlefield Street, Avon, MA 02322 U.S.A.
www.adamsmedia.com

ISBN-13: 978-1-59869-614-1
ISBN-10: 1-59869-614-9

Printed in Canada.

J I H G F E D C B A

Library of Congress Cataloging-in-Publication Data
available from the publisher.

Contains material adopted and abridged from
The Everything® Paying for College Book by Nathan Brown and
Sheryle A. Proper, Copyright © 2005 by F+W Publications, Inc.

This publication is designed to provide accurate and authoritative information with regard to the subject matter covered. It is sold with the understanding that the publisher is not engaged in rendering legal, accounting,
or other professional advice. If legal advice or other expert assistance
is required, the services of a competent professional person should be
sought.

— From a *Declaration of Principles* jointly adopted
by a Committee of the American Bar Association
and a Committee of Publishers and Associations

Many of the designations used by manufacturers and sellers to distinguish
their product are claimed as trademarks. Where those designations appear
in this book and Adams Media was aware of a trademark claim, the designations have been printed with initial capital letters.

*This book is available at quantity discounts for bulk purchases.
For information, please call 1-800-289-0963.*

CONTENTS

INTRODUCTION

By now you know, whether you're a parent or a student—after high school comes college. A college education offers possibility, it is the path to a better understanding of the world, it is preparation for bigger and better things, it is preparation to have a positive impact in the lives of others, and it holds the promise of financial security. Right?

So here you are, you picked up this book because either you, or someone you know and care about, is about to take the plunge. Choosing to attend college is a life-changing decision and a huge financial commitment. Nervous yet? You're not alone. Going to college can be affordable—and with *Mr. Cheap's Guide to Paying for College,* you'll learn how to milk your money, work the system, get through college without going broke.

Everybody's got questions! If you're the student: Where should I apply? What should I major in? If you're the parent: How can I pay for it? Drum roll, please . . . college is expensive! In fact, few things have increased in cost in the past few decades as much as college tuition.

But people figure out a way to find the money to get through college every day. Do they come out of school saddled with debt? Do they struggle through on soup and energy bars? Do they even enjoy their experience? With this book, you'll be smarter!

Planning is the first step, so good for you. But how exactly can you go to the school that you know is right for you but seems out of your financial means? If you really want that education, then this book will show you how it is possible. You can get that degree and not be in debt more than what is necessary to springboard you into your potential future.

There are dozens of sources of financial aid, hundreds of ways to cut back on costs, and thousands of ways to save money. *Mr. Cheap's Guide to Paying for College* will get you started. It will inspire you to use the methods outlined here, and it will prompt you to use creative thinking to discover even more sources of "free money." Financing the high cost of a college education starts today. Just think—if you learn how to manage your money now and get a great education at the same time, you will be so ahead of the game come graduation day! There is a school, somewhere, that fits your ability, your talents, your interests, your skills, *and* your financial boundaries. Now is the time to start figuring it all out.

chapter 1

WHAT'S IT GONNA COST YOU?

If you want to be ready for the outrageous costs of college, then you'd better know what you're in for and be prepared. Taking action before you go to college is the way to avoid what could otherwise become a serious cash strain. College is a time when your focus should be on academics, not on how to pay for your education! But let's be honest, if you can't figure out a way to pay then you can't go to college—so let's get started!

MR. CHEAP'S

$

THE RISING COST OF TUITION

In the academic year 2006–2007, the average cost for two full-time semesters at a two-year public college, including tuition and fees, was approximately $2,272. At public four-year institutions (which approximately 80 percent of all students attend) the average cost per year was about $5,836. The cost of attending a four-year private institution ran to more than $22,000.

During the 2006–2007 school year, 42 percent of all full-time undergraduate-level college students attended schools with tuition and fees of less than $6,000 per year. Thirteen percent of undergraduate students that year attended private institutions with fees of $24,000 or more. It's bad, I know—but not unmanageable. Don't stop reading yet!

Current Tuition Cost Increases

In the 2006–2007 academic year, the collective costs of fees and tuition, when viewed as a percentage increase from the previous year, have gone through the roof. The cost at a four-year public university jumped more than 6 percent from the previous year. Attending a private institution ran just shy of $23,000, an increase of almost 6 percent.

Multiply those increases by four years and you have a hefty sum of money, no matter what type of institution you are considering.

Don't Forget About Room and Board

Room and board, room and board. You will soon be sick of this phrase because it is repeated again and again as you read through the pages of this book. But the truth is college students do more than just attend classes at college! And sometimes, it's all those other costs that put people over the edge. Most of the time, students live on campus—which can be a big expense. In fact, some schools even require starting freshmen to live in the dorms. In 2006, the average American college student paid between $340 and $390 more (compared to 2005) for on-campus room and board, depending on the type and location of the college they were attending. At public universities in 2006–2007, students paid an extra $6,960 for two-year colleges and $8,149 (a $386 increase from 2005) for four-year private colleges, on top of tuition and academic fees.

CHEAP$KATE

The cost of college tuition rises every single year. It's important to think about this when you visit colleges. During your visit, be sure to ask by what percentage their tuition has increased over the past few years. Be prepared for a scary answer but hey, let's try to think about the bright side. Ha!—you say, but you may be able to qualify for additional financial aid that will help cover some of these increases!

Difference in Tuition Increases from State to State

The *where* factor is a big part of the college decision. Since recent tuition and fee increases differ from state to state, let's take a state-by-state look. The following list shows the percentage by which college tuition and fees increased from the academic year 2005–2006 to 2006–2007.

INCREASE IN ANNUAL TUITION AND FEES AT PUBLIC INSTITUTIONS FROM 2005–2006 TO 2006–2007

STATE	FOUR-YEAR INSTITUTIONS	TWO-YEAR INSTITUTIONS
National Average	6%	4%
Alabama	5%	<1%
Alaska	10%	10%
Arizona	6%	7%
Arkansas	6%	7%
California	1%	–10%
Colorado	5%	3%
Connecticut	6%	5%
Delaware	6%	7%
Florida	4%	6%
Georgia	6%	5%
Hawaii	22%	13%
Idaho	6%	5%
Illinois	12%	8%
Indiana	6%	6%
Iowa	5%	4%
Kansas	11%	2%
Kentucky	12%	11%
Louisiana	4%	1%
Maine	8%	9%
Maryland	1%	2%
Massachusetts	4%	1%
Michigan	7%	6%
Minnesota	8%	7%
Mississippi	6%	1%

STATE	FOUR-YEAR INSTITUTIONS	TWO-YEAR INSTITUTIONS
Missouri	5%	2%
Montana	8%	5%
Nebraska	6%	7%
Nevada	9%	3%
New Hampshire	6%	<1%
New Jersey	9%	8%
New Mexico	7%	6%
New York	1%	2%
North Carolina	10%	1%
North Dakota	9%	7%
Ohio	6%	6%
Oklahoma	11%	4%
Oregon	5%	6%
Pennsylvania	5%	4%
Rhode Island	6%	9%
South Carolina	7%	5%
South Dakota	7%	7%
Tennessee	4%	5%
Texas	8%	6%
Utah	8%	9%
Vermont	5%	5%
Virginia	9%	8%
Washington	7%	6%
West Virginia	7%	4%
Wisconsin	7%	8%
Wyoming	3%	3%

Figures from the Trends in College Pricing, Trends in Higher Education Series 2006 by CollegeBoard.

Whether the tuition in your state increased by a lot or a little, students across the country are in the same boat. Tuition increased in all fifty states! And tuition costs are going to get even higher before they start to get better. But there *are* ways to make it work.

CHEAP$KATE

Many students actually pay less than the published costs! Find out what you'll *really* pay, the net cost to you, by boldly but nicely asking what scholarships and grants are available at each school and how you can get them.

IS IT WORTH THE PRICE OF ADMISSION?

At this point you may be asking yourself if the high cost of tuition is really worth it. And the answer is: absolutely! Statistics show that more often than not, money spent for a college education is money well spent. On average, you can expect your annual salary to be about $18,000 greater compared to what you would make if you only had a high school diploma. Over a lifetime, a bachelor's degree (or a master's and/or doctorate) is worth more than $1 million more than you could expect to earn if your education stops after high school. This difference grows even bigger if you have earned a degree in a high-tech or computer-related field.

CHEAP$KATE

Need some more convincing? Well, consider this: according to statistics from the U.S. Census Bureau, Americans with a bachelor's degree earn 60 percent more, on average, than Americans with high school diplomas!

MORE THAN JUST TUITION

First of all, let's consider the differences between the "comprehensive fees" at the institution in question and the total "cost of attendance." This is important! Comprehensive fees include things that the school will actually include on your bill. Most of the time, these fees include standard college basics such as tuition, mandatory fees (computing access fee, student activities fee, and so on), on-campus housing (residence hall or dormitory), and the dining-hall meal plan. The actual cost of attendance, on the other hand, includes the total for all estimated college costs. Calculating this total cost of attendance sets the limit on what you will be able to receive in financial aid from the school you plan to attend.

Every year, or even every quarter, college financial aid officers consider various elements to estimate the total cost of attendance at their institutions. This could be considered as the average student's budget. Factors that are considered often include the following:

- Tuition and fees
- Room-and-board expenses
- Textbooks, supplies, and personal expenses
- Transportation (gas, public transit, and so on)
- Dependent-care expenses
- Disability-related expenses
- Study-abroad expenses
- Employment-related expenses related to co-op educational programs
- Student loan fees

It's important to remember that not all schools include the same costs in their calculations. University administrators are often required to set reasonable cost boundaries when determining these budget components. They are not, however, under any obligation to include all the above-mentioned categories when calculating their institution's official total cost of attendance.

One institution's total may include the costs of study-abroad expenses, for instance, while another institution may exclude them, every institution is different. At an institution with very few older or returning students, administrators probably won't include dependent-care expenses in their total cost of attendance, nor will they likely have any co-op educational programs. Keep in mind that these budget items are calculated for the average student's cost of attendance. You may spend more or less than the totals determined by the standard budgeted amounts. But it's key to keep these costs in mind when you're looking at multiple schools.

COMPARING SCHOOLS BY COST

It's not easy, but it will be worth it. Because schools don't always include the same items in their calculations of total attendance costs, you should be careful to make an "apples-to-apples" comparison when you are ready to evaluate the costs of different institutions. In other words, match them up element for element, not just cost for cost. If you simply compare different schools in terms of their total estimated cost of attendance, you are assuming that textbook prices, supply costs, and personal expenses are the same, regardless of which schools are being compared—and this is not always the case. Some things simply cost more at different schools or in different areas of the country.

You will also need to make your own adjustments to an institution's budgeted amounts according to your individual situation. If you live on the West Coast and are considering a number of different colleges, some in California and some on the other side of the country, your actual transportation costs will vary greatly depending on the school's distance from home.

Just an Estimate, Please

For a rough estimate of cost comparison, it is okay to compare totals rather than itemize everything specifically. If you feel that you must compare totals, however, the key is consistency! Compare one school's comprehensive fees to the other's, or examine total costs of attendance, but don't mix up the two. If you compare comprehensive fees at NYU to the total cost of attendance at Berkeley, for example, you are going to end up with confusing and misleading results.

Don't Be Scared Off by High Costs!

Okay, so you did your "apples-to-apples" . . . next! But before you cross anything off your list, neither parents nor students should rule out any institution simply because of its high cost of attendance. There still may be a way to work it out! Financial aid programs are designed to make the dream of college a reality—even when you dream big. The better prepared for college the student is, and the more the family learns about preparing for and paying the costs, the more opportunities and options will become available at any institution.

The amount of financial aid a student receives can vary tremendously from one institution to the next. Therefore, financial concerns should not really come into play until the student is ready to make that final college choice. For example, state universities usually have much lower comprehensive fees than private institutions. After you calculate the value of scholarships and/or grants you may be awarded at that school, you might find that the private school's net cost is lower than the net cost of a state institution, even though the cost of attendance is much higher.

LEARNING TO LIVE ON LESS

Even after running all the numbers, you shouldn't consider your calculation of the cost of attending a particular school to be set in stone. Two students attending the same institution may end up with very different actual costs of attendance. Why? Because depending on a number of factors, the cost of living can vary from person to person. For instance, a student's eating habits may be affected by a wide range of factors, like personal preference, health concerns, religion, the student's accustomed standard of living, and even the student's size and appetite. Schools may charge higher tuition for out-of-state students, and students who live on campus may have different costs of attendance than students who choose to live off campus. Remember, the money that a student must actually spend is not necessarily factored into an institution's official cost of attendance, so you need to make these calculations on your own.

Personal Cost-of-Living Factors

What specific aspects of your lifestyle will affect your wallet when you go off to college? Can you curb the more expensive habits? Or are your preferences set in stone? Think about it . . .

- If you're an Orthodox Jew, you will only be able to eat food that is kosher. Unless your university has a dining hall dedicated to making dishes that meet kosher dietary requirements, you will probably have to spend money out-of-pocket in order to eat meals in accordance with religious doctrine.
- You may be used to getting your hair cut or styled every week, or maybe every other week. While living at home, your parents probably paid this expense. At college, however, you will need to either cut down on the frequency of your hair appointments or allot money for this extra expense.

"Consumable" Cost of Living

Many of the things college students spend money on are classified as consumables. The "consumables" category includes things like convenience foods, along with other quick-and-easy items commonly found in grocery and drug stores. At the Economic Research Institute's Web site (*www.erieri.com*), you can use a student cost-of-living calculator that lets you compare any school location's estimated cost of consumables to the national average. After you choose the city where your university or college of choice is located, the calculator will provide you with a consumable percentage of the national average. This consumable percentage is based upon the assumptions that you are employed and earning at least the minimum wage, are sharing your apartment with roommates, and are paying at least minimum federal and state taxes. But are you doing all these things? No? Maybe you should!

CHEAP$KATE

Get it in your head now that getting a degree is the main reason you are going to college. Ask yourself, "Do I really need this?" before spending any money on non-tuition items.

The impact of consumables upon living expenses varies with each student's level of earnings. For example, your consumable expenses may account for just 20 percent of your income, while your roommate and best friend spends a whopping 50 percent. Cost of living depends heavily on the kind of expenditure decisions you make, such as the size and type of your residence, as well as on expenses like income taxes, cost of services, transportation costs, and other miscellaneous items.

Common Non-Tuition Expenses

There are three general expenses not related to tuition that you should definitely keep in mind as you estimate what your cost of living will be while at college. In the world of college costs, the "biggies" to consider are:

Transportation: If you do not plan to live in the on-campus dormitory—or at least within walking distance of your campus—plan on adding a minimum of $75 a month to your living expenses. This figure will vary. For instance, will you take public transportation or keep your own car (with associated insurance, parking, gas, and maintenance fees)? Be sure to take all costs into account—bus pass or on-campus parking permit—and figure on contingencies like whether you drive yourself or make car pool arrangements.

Books and Supplies: You should plan to spend about $1,000 on textbooks and general supplies each year. If you plan to study a specialized, technical subject (math and sciences, for instance), or if you plan to study subjects requiring special materials (film, fine arts), you may want to allot additional funds for the purchase of specialized textbooks as well as course-specific instruments and supplies.

Board and Lodging: Depending on your choice of meal plan and the availability of rooms on campus, costs for room and board can range as high as $4,500 to $8,000 or more per year. If you plan to live in the dorm, or even in an apartment, you should plan to spend approximately $135 per week to keep a roof over your head and food in your stomach.

Still not convinced that these things will run up your expenses *that much*? Keep reading.

HOW MUCH FOR ALL OF THIS?

In 1998, the national average cost for a college textbook was $61.50. This represented an increase of $4 from the previous year, according to the National Association of College Stores. In recent years, textbook costs have grown much higher. In fact, prices have gone up so much that they have raised national attention—to the point that consumers have even called for the government to investigate!

Survey of Textbook Costs

To find out how much students really spend on textbooks, the California Student Public Interest Research Group (CALPIRG), Oregon Student Public Interest Research Group (OSPIRG), and the OSPIRG Foundation conducted a survey. They looked at the most widely required college textbooks during the fall semester of 2003 at ten public colleges and state universities in both California and Oregon. More than 150 faculty members and more than 500 students were interviewed about the cost of textbooks and individual purchasing preferences. The main findings of the survey were are follows:

- College students spent an average of $898 per year on both new and used textbooks in 2003–2004. This represents nearly 20 percent of the average tuition and fees for in-state students at public four-year colleges nationwide. (An earlier survey at the same schools found that in 1996–1997, the average cost of textbooks was $642.)
- Roughly 50 percent of college-level textbooks now come in bundled packages or have been shrink-

wrapped with additional materials (such as interactive CD-ROMs or supplemental workbooks). Students are often not given the option of buying these textbooks without the additional materials, even if they do not plan or need to use them.

- In only one instance was a textbook available in both bundled and unbundled (textbook only) packages. The bundled version cost more than two times as much as the unbundled version of the same college textbook.

- Approximately 65 percent of professors and college instructors said they rarely made use of the bundled packages' extra materials in their college courses.

- According to 76 percent of professors and instructors, new editions of textbooks were "never" to "half the time" justified. A full 40 percent of professors and instructors reported that the new college textbook editions were "rarely" to "never" justified.

- New college textbooks cost an average of $102. This is 58 percent more expensive than the average price of used textbooks, which is close to $65.

- Of college students who specifically wanted used textbooks, 59 percent were unable to find even one used textbook for their entire schedule of classes.

CHEAP$KATE

Why is it more expensive for some? Costs can vary depending on the type of class (with science books tending to cost more than other disciplines), the number of books each professor requires, and whether the student can find any used copies. Seems like there's not much you can do about these things, huh? Well, that's not necessarily true! Keep reading.

Recent Development

In 2006, the Senior Republican Member of the U.S. House Education and Labor Committee, Rep. Howard P. "Buck" McKeon, asked the Advisory Committee on Student Financial Assistance to report on the continuing higher cost of college textbooks. Rep. McKeon commented on the report findings on May 30, 2007. He said, "I am pleased that institutions and publishers are beginning to tackle this issue on behalf of students and parents alike." Among it's recommendations, the Advisory Committee encourages institutions to provide more used textbooks, allow for textbook rentals, and create programs to help students pay for textbooks.

School Supplies

Keep in mind that you will also be spending money on school supplies. By "school supplies," we mean more than just pencils, pens, paper, and the other usual stuff you geared up with during your high school years. Remember, as a college student, you will be doing more than simply going to classes—you will probably live there as well. So it is important for you to bring the right kind of gear for the job. By doing this, you can save yourself a lot of money in the long run.

Buy Certain Items in Advance

Don't forget—it is almost always easier to find things cheaper in your own hometown than it will be at the on-campus store of a new school. Of course, you will first need to know what to buy. Don't rush around without a plan and start impulse buying, wasting money on a bunch of things you will probably not even need.

For example, the cost of residence hall rooms may include use of a small refrigerator or microwave. Before you go out and purchase these items, find out from the institution's residential life office if these amenities are included or whether you can rent them.

CHEAP$KATE

When that orientation info comes in the mail, use it! Look at what your new college provides in the dorms and call up your future roomie! Coordinating your needs before you even leave for move-in day will save you money! You should check to see whether your roommate has already bought a fridge or microwave that you might be able to share, or if these items are even allowed in your dorm! If you must buy these items, watch the classified ads and buy used if you can.

To give you an idea of the kinds of things you should plan to buy in advance, here are some essential items that most college students will want to have:

Shower bucket/tote—This handy carryall can be rolled or carried from a student's room to the bathroom. (In dorms, students may share a bathroom with quite a few people.) If you leave things sitting unsupervised in a community bathroom, they could get stolen. Or worse, someone you do not know (and do not want to share hygiene products with) will use them.

Cheap, nonperishable food items—We all get hungry sometimes, and the dining hall isn't always open. Peanut butter, macaroni and cheese, and dry cereal are all good to have in a dorm room. They won't go bad and stink up the room. You can also consider drink options like instant coffee, tea bags, hot cocoa mix, or Kool-Aid.

Does your family buy items in bulk? Stock up before you leave home! The more necessary items you bring with you to college, the less you will have to buy later. It would be wise to make a list of these items and take at least a shopping day or two to locate and purchase them in advance.

Writing materials—This includes an address book, stationery, spiral notebooks and notebook paper, envelopes (and postage stamps).

Stuff to eat/drink with—Find a cheap plastic bowl, reusable (yet disposable) plate, fork and spoon, large plastic cup, mug for coffee, and a travel mug if you plan to take that coffee to class (spilled coffee in class is a quick way to get on the professor's bad side).

Clothes-drying rack—Dormitory dryers do not always work. Sometimes they work a little too well. Apart from the fact that they do not always perform as you would like, they usually cost money to use. A drying rack can help you save your money and your clothes.

Plastic basin—This can be used as a second sink or just as a dirty dish holder (but definitely not for both purposes simultaneously).

Write-on/wipe-off board—Messages are often unreliable when left in a dorm, and your answering machines won't help if someone stops by your room and you're not around. One of those small dry-erase boards posted on or by your dorm room door is a great way for your friends to leave messages when you're out of the room.

Laundry bag or basket—You'll need one of these to carry your laundry to and from the laundry room.

Remember, laundry baskets work better if you actually fold the laundry once it's done.

Alarm clock—Be sure you buy one with a snooze button. As a college student, you don't have the luxury of mumbling "Just five more minutes, Mom."

"Plasti-tac" putty—This stuff is great for hanging things on your dorm room walls. Colleges usually do not allow tape or nails to be used for hanging posters, pictures, plaques, and so on. If you plan to get an off-campus apartment, it will be easier to get your security deposit back if you haven't put a lot of holes in the walls.

Flashlight and extra batteries—Blackouts can happen.

Mini medicine cabinet—Include a small box of aspirin, cold/flu medicine, band-aids, and so on. Moms feel better knowing their students have these items with them.

These things will be cheapest at your local thrift store or the dollar store—you're not looking for quality here, as the odds are good that you won't have any of them for very long. In fact, you shouldn't bring anything with you to college that you are not willing to have lost, stolen, broken, warped, or otherwise ruined and tossed out.

CHEAP$KATE

Don't fall into the "convenience" trap and pay three to four times more for essential items at convenience stores that can be bought at discount stores. One of your first orientation activities when you first arrive to campus should be to find the discount stores in your college town.

Be Resourceful

As a student, you should take advantage of the opportunities available on campus for getting "free" school supplies. You can often get free pencils and pens from clubs, organizations, student government officers, and other groups that are recruiting, campaigning, or just trying to get publicity. There are also places where you can use supplies without having to buy them yourself. Libraries often have a stapler, hole punch, and other such items that you can drop by and use. (Students should remember to *use* these items, not *steal* them.)

CHEAP$KATE

Once again, if you plan it, you can do it. Like when your friends are going out to eat, but for the student on a budget, dining out regularly is costly. If you put aside a small amount of money each week, you can probably swing these outings without going broke.

Other Possible Incidental Expenses

Additional expenses aside from tuition that may not be included in the cost of attendance are music lesson fees, course lab and other special class fees, computer-related expenses, and pizza money.

In addition to the costs of basic room and board, off-campus lodging, and tuition, you must also consider incidental expenses when estimating the total cost for a year of attendance at a university or college. The general range of incidental expenses commonly runs between $1,800 and $2,000 a year. This covers items we've already discussed, such as books and supplies, as well as personal expenses for laundry, cleaning, recreation, and minor clothing replacements. You should also budget premiums for accident and health insurance, which is highly recommended.

Remember that incidental expenses for a college education will vary according to your tastes and the activities you participate in. Costs for items such as laundry, personal needs, and entertainment will vary according to individual preferences. If you take courses in graphic arts, painting, sculpting, and the like, the cost of your course supplies may be somewhat higher. Students who plan to join fraternities, sororities, honor societies, or certain student groups will have to factor in dues, social events, honor banquets, and other possible incidentals that come with membership.

Chapter 2

GET READY TO MAKE SOME IMPORTANT CHOICES

Before you can start heading in the right direction, it's necessary to have a general idea of where you want to end up. Both students and parents need to think about what makes an ideal school—for starters, you may want to focus on the student's interests and personal strengths. Using those as a springboard, do some research and come up with a list of colleges you're interested in. You can base your choices on institution size, majors offered, or distance from home—whatever is most important to you and/or your student.

IDENTIFY YOUR STRENGTHS

Take a moment to think about strengths. If you're the kind of student who scores high in language classes such as English or Spanish, and you are active in dance, art, or drama, then schools with good liberal arts programs would be a natural choice for starting out your search for potential colleges. If you get very high grades in mathematics and science classes, and you were good at advanced subjects like calculus, computer programming, and/or physics (classes many high school students never take because they get stuck at the lower levels), then a more technical school that focuses on fields related to math and science may be an excellent choice for you. Of course, expanding your interests and abilities can give you a big advantage over other people in the job market when you graduate, so don't be afraid to consider schools that can accommodate <u>all</u> of your interests, skills, and talents. Look for schools that have opportunities for you to grow and excel in more than one area. College is a place to experiment and look into things that you might not normally have a chance to. Broaden your horizons! You might find you like science when you thought you hated it . . . hey—you never know!

Stay Ahead of the Game

Pay attention to ratings and rankings of colleges and universities, but do not put too much emphasis on them when making your decision. There are other factors, such as campus life, internship options, and activities that each individual student should consider.

Once you have identified strengths, weaknesses, and interests, it is time to start looking. Maybe you already have some schools in mind. Write them down, and start a list of schools to research further. Ask your school guidance counselor for advice on schools that might fit your strengths and interests. You can also go online and search for schools by the program or major you are interested in. Using any search engine, such as Google or Yahoo, type in your search keywords as follows: "college university [name of major] major."

YOU KNOW WHAT'S FREE? INFORMATION!

The only thing that comes free when it comes to college is information. Schools are more than happy to send prospective students all the information they possibly can—all you have to do is ask. Once you have a list of possible schools, it's time to find out all you can about each and every one of them. All you have to do is request an information packet from the school's admissions office. Even better, many schools now honor e-mail requests for information. Just go to the school's Web site to find out if they offer this option. Remember that the best decision is an informed decision. The information is free, and the schools are happy to give it to you, so there is no excuse for not requesting these useful little packets from all the schools on your list.

Better to See It Yourself

Visit as many of the schools you're interested in as you can. If you are a traditional student, the college you attend will most likely become your home away from home for most of the academic year. If all goes as planned, it will continue to be home for the next four years. Think about it like this—would you purchase a house and move in without ever having taken a look at it? Almost anyone would want to at least glance inside. In the same way, you want to make sure that you will be comfortable enough at your school that you can be an efficient student.

SAVVY STUDENTS SAVE

If you can't travel to a school because of time, cost, or other reasons, consider a cyber tour. Many schools now have quality online tours that give you a real feel for the campus without leaving your home. It's a great way to get an overview of the physical campus.

If you feel terribly overwhelmed during a short visit, you can just imagine how you might feel later—weeks into the semester, after you factor in the stress of classes and homework every day. On the other hand, don't underestimate your adaptation skills, either. (Think back to how intimidating your high school was at the beginning of your freshman year compared to how you see it now.) Just be sure you have an idea what you are getting yourself into. If you fall in love with a school at first sight, you may know it's the one for you; if it's not even close to what was represented in the brochures, you may end up crossing it off your list. This is why it's important to keep your options open and visit as many schools as you can.

You'd Better Learn to Love Paperwork

Gather your financial aid information (the school needs data for you and your parents), so you will have it together and ready when you need to complete certain financial aid forms. This includes copies of federal tax returns, particularly for the year before the one when you plan to enter college. Necessary papers may also include (but are not limited to) W-2 income statements, receipts for cash income, personal savings records, bank account statements, social security benefit statements, and investment accounts. You may want to call each school's financial aid office to find out what other paperwork they require. You do not want find yourself at the financial aid office with a pile of papers only to be told, "There is another form you forgot. You will have to fill this out and come back later."

Get yourself a file folder (one that can be securely closed with a clasp or tie) and keep your important financial notes, statements, and papers in it. Be meticulous about this—if you take papers out, put them back as soon as you are done with them or if you will not need them for more than an hour. This prevents papers from being lost or accidentally discarded. Mark the folder with a label like "Important Papers!" or "Do Not Throw Away!"

Stay Ahead of the Game

Regional colleges tend to attract students from the college's immediate geographic region. These candidates are generally well-prepared for college. National liberal arts colleges tend to admit students from wider geographic and social backgrounds who have exceptionally strong academic backgrounds. They emphasize undergraduate education and may or may not offer graduate programs.

Ask the Right Questions or You'll Be Sorry

Before you go off to make a serious visit to a prospective university or college campus, you should be sure you have completed all the required forms by the set deadlines. During your visit, or even by phone before you go, you should make sure to ask questions such as those found in the following list:

- When is your admissions application deadline?
- What financial aid forms do you require, and what are the deadlines?
- What types of financial aid do you offer to students?
- Is there a separate application for academic scholarships?
- Are any types of financial aid "guaranteed?"
- When can I expect to receive my financial aid package?

Do not rest until all of your questions have been answered to your full satisfaction. Avoid the possibility of "bad-rumor syndrome" or of misinformation by always making an effort to ask the appropriate people the appropriate questions. Don't be afraid to ask someone to explain something again or in more detail—college cost is a big thing and you deserve to know (and understand) what you're getting yourself and your family into!

Stay Ahead of the Game

Ask your student tour guide or other students you see on campus the questions only students can answer. For example, "How do you like going to school here?" or "How's the cafeteria food?"

Don't Let the Shiny Luster Blind You

It is very easy to allow yourself to become distracted by the "glamour and glitter" that many universities put on during special visit programs and campus visitor tours for prospective students. You should decide by seeing, not by being told. As far as the school is concerned, there is a good reason to stage this kind of show—they want you to see their school in its best light so you will want to go there. More students means more money for them. Some schools think convincing you means selling the idea of their school to you in very much the same way a door-to-door vacuum cleaner salesman tries to convince you to buy a $1,500 machine—by making it look new, putting on some shiny stuff, and showing you all the cool parts.

Visiting a campus is definitely the best way to get to know what that college or university is really like. However, you must fight to resist the "shiny" spell that they are trying to cast on you. Do not allow yourself (whether you are a parent or a student) to become entranced into making a rash commitment because of a tour. Remember, unless you stick to your guns and ask all the right questions, most college tours will show you the best parts of the campus, and a lot of window dressing. Stay focused on the reasons you decided to make this visit in the first place. Arrange in advance to sit in on a real class if you can, or make an appointment to visit a professor or two in your areas of academic interest. Having a meal in the dining hall is also a good idea.

Stay Ahead of the Game

Be prepared to get all the details when visiting a campus. Ask questions like, "Where is it?" "How many are there?" "What kind?" "How often?" "Who is allowed?" "When is it open?" Go ahead, be a pest. Do this and you will get a better sense of "what am I paying for?"

A very good method for avoiding becoming blinded by the shiny luster is to make a list of things you want to see, do, and find out about. You will decide in advance on some of the items on your list based on your wants and needs. Other items will be based on statements your tour guide makes as you go along. Don't trust all the fancy descriptions, and make notes of things you want to investigate on your own. For example, a school may boast having "an extensive library and numerous computer labs around campus." Remember that these are vague descriptions, and one person's idea of "extensive" or "numerous" may not be another's. That extensive library may seem smaller in real life than it does in the school's representation—but you won't know this unless you make the effort to see it for yourself.

The guide may even tell you that "numerous computer labs" means four labs that serve the campus. That sounds like a lot of computers, doesn't it? Well, it could be that two of those labs only have a dozen stations. If the tour guide takes you to the main computer lab (which is the big lab that schools often show on tours), remember to ask where students can find additional labs. The tour guide may tell you, "Our campus has three more facilities that are like this one." Well, that may be true—but you won't know just how much "like this one" those other facilities are until you have physically laid eyes upon them. If this would be a selling point for you, be sure to check it out for yourself.

You're Not Done! Your Visit Isn't Over Until You Write It Down

Create a college cost comparison and financial aid worksheet when you get home from your first college visit. Add information to your worksheet after each additional visit. Keep in mind that books, transportation, and personal expenses will not be included in your bill. In fact, the actual expenses will also vary according to your distance from the college you plan to attend and to your personal choices (and whether they are wise ones). Compare the costs of tuition, fees, housing, and meal plans for each of the colleges you visit. Add some rough estimates for variable expenses such as books, transportation, and personal expenses to each. Once that has been done, subtract the financial aid you are eligible to receive at each school. Here is an example of a college cost and financial aid comparison worksheet:

COLLEGE COST COMPARISON WORKSHEET				
COST	COLLEGE A	COLLEGE B	COLLEGE C	COLLEGE D
Tuition				
Mandatory fees				
Housing				
Meal plans				
Total Billable Costs				
Books				
Transportation				
Personal expenses				
Total cost of attendance				
Less financial aid package				
Equals net cost to student				

Please take note that you will probably have to apply for admission at your chosen schools and be accepted before you can get a financial aid package. Most colleges only determine financial aid eligibility after a student has been accepted for admission. Go ahead and do all of the financial aid paperwork for all potential institutions before their set deadlines, even if you if you have not received an official letter of acceptance or admission from them just yet. The admissions and financial aid processes are separate, so get a good start on each one.

ARE YOU READY FOR COLLEGE?

Once you have received information from all schools, you may find that some are obvious standouts—they have the program or major you're interested in, a great location, and the kind of campus life you're looking for. If you feel this good about a school, go ahead and start working on an application. What are you waiting for? The sooner you get that app in, the sooner you will learn about financial aid and the sooner you can include that piece in your decision of where to go.

College visits are a good way of making sure that a school is as wonderful as it sounds in those official brochures you've been reading. If you're still unsure about a school, you might as well wait to apply until you can make a visit. But remember, just because you apply to a certain school does not mean you have to go there. The sooner you apply, the sooner the school will make an admissions decision and then send you information about the financial aid possibilities they can offer you if you are accepted.

What Are You Waiting For?

If you are a person who likes to start things off already in the lead position, you may want to think about applying for early admission. If you are a procrastinator, it's a good idea to get started right now! There are commonly two avenues of attack for people who want to get a jump on things. The first is called early action.

Early action is an admissions option that binds the university or college to the student applicant, but it does not bind the applicant to the school. What does this mean to you as a student? It means that if the school accepts you for admission, and you pay a deposit, the school is left with no choice but to let you in when your first semester rolls around. However, you are able to retain your power of choice and may go to college somewhere else should you decide to do so (although you will probably have to forfeit your deposit).

Stay Ahead of the Game

Make 100 percent sure that you know which schools offer what options before you sign any early option contract and pay a deposit. Also make sure that you are fully aware of the dates for all early paperwork (or other) deadlines.

The second avenue of attack is called early decision. An early decision admission option is a little more restrictive, as it is binding for both the school and the applicant. This means that if you are accepted and you pay your deposit, then you and the school have a contractual agreement that you are not only admitted, you will definitely attend. You must withdraw your applications at all other schools. Although it commits you to attend that institution, at least for the first semester, it's a terrific option if you are sure that is the school you want to attend. The pressure is off students because the decision is made early enough to really enjoy the rest of your senior year of high school. That gives the student and parents peace of mind.

First Come, First Served?

Even if you don't think early admission is for you, you still have no excuse for unnecessary procrastination. Students and parents should plan to get regular applications to the post office ahead of deadline time. This is the best way of making sure there will be placements available. Didn't expect that one, did you? Well, believe it or not, certain schools operate on a "first come, first serve" basis of admission. This is technically known as a "rolling admission" policy. Instead of waiting for the deadline to pass and evaluating all applications, admissions officers look at each application as it arrives. As students are accepted, spots are assigned in the incoming class. If any of the schools on your list uses this method, it's important to send your applications off as early as you can (as long as you don't drive yourself crazy in the process!). Even if the school has a set admissions deadline instead of a rolling one, you should get your application in early. That gives you more time to collect any missing documents necessary to complete your application packet. Schools are not likely to start reviewing your application until all required forms, recommendation letters, essays, and transcripts have been received.

MANAGE YOUR ACTIVITIES

Admissions committees are seeking more than just students with good grades. They are also eager to recruit students who are outstanding in other ways. Don't make the mistake of thinking you're an automatic "in" because you list a number of activities on your application and are therefore "well rounded." Most of the time, admissions officers are actually in search of students who as a group will make up a well-rounded population. In other words, they're looking for a diverse array of individuals with many different types of interests and abilities. By doing this, they are able to attract the interest and attention of more potential students for the future. Remember that while colleges do have minimum standards for student admissions, they have to bring in money. Some institutions do not want to grow larger and purposely keep their enrollment at a certain level. However a smaller student body than whatever the target class size is means a smaller amount of tuition being paid out by the student body as a whole—something that all college administrators definitely wish to avoid.

This myth-busting truth is not necessarily a bad thing. It prevents you from having to type up a multipage list of activities to accompany your application essays, including things like the Underwater Basket-Weaving Club and the Eating Utensil Band. (Unless examples like these qualify as your primary activity, you can probably leave them out.)

However, this does not mean that you should cut down on the number of activities you participate in simply because you are concerned it will make you look bad on paper. There is a difference between applicants who are just trying to beef up their profiles by increasing the quantity of their memberships and applicants who have excelled in only a few activities—and college admissions officers have a lot of experience in telling that difference.

Stay Ahead of the Game

Though it is wise to have a broad scope of extracurricular activities, too many can cause admissions administrators to view you as unfocused, erratic, or spreading yourself too thin. This is not to say you should eliminate activities you love. Instead, you should be sure you love the activities you do. If you love one activity, and you are successful doing it, you might get a scholarship for it! But remember, there aren't any scholarships for "scatterbrains!"

You should not start stressing yourself out by trying to join clubs and organizations that you believe (or have heard) college admissions officers want to see listed on applications. You should do your best to avoid allowing such assumptions to control your choice of activities. It makes a lot more sense to concentrate on those activities that you are truly, passionately interested in, and strive to do your very best at them.

KEYS TO ADMISSION—THE INTERVIEW AND THE ESSAY

Though they are not required as often as they were in past years, a face-to-face interview can serve as a second chance for students to sell themselves to the admissions office.

Some students have even begun requesting personal interviews in the hopes that the extra effort will increase their chances for acceptance. Some, however, would just like an opportunity to get a firsthand look at the campus. For whatever reason, if you plan to go to an interview, you will need to be prepared.

You can usually visit a campus on whatever day works best for you, although you may want to try to schedule these interviews for either a Monday or a Friday. This way, you, and perhaps even your parents, will be able to spend some leisurely time on campus the weekend before or after the interview.

SAVVY STUDENTS SAVE

If you and your family are unfamiliar with the area and do not know anyone at or near that school, it is a good idea to contact the admissions office so they can help you make arrangements for multiple-day visits. Many universities now have overnight visiting programs for prospective students. Don't pay for a hotel room when you can visit with a student and learn the lay of the land—for free!

As for the interview itself, the best thing for both you and your parents to do is to take it easy. Don't forget—you are there to find out more about the school. You are the one who has to decide if you even want to go to this school. The school is trying just as hard to make an impression on you as you are on them.

Both students and parents need to be on their best behavior when visiting a school. Dress well, have a few intelligent questions in mind (about subjects important to you), use a firm (though not vise-like) handshake, and always talk and act like you know what you're doing—even when

GET READY TO MAKE SOME IMPORTANT CHOICES

you don't. Rehearsal interviews can also be a good prep tool, either with a parent or a teacher or guidance counselor.

The All-Important Essay

Your grade point average, name and address, and your SAT or ACT score do not give admissions officers any relevant information about the kind of human being you are or how you spend your time. This is why school admissions offices often ask for essays to accompany student applications. This is your big chance to dazzle them by showing them who you are and what you have done in life. However, you must not try to make yourself sound like anyone other than who you really are (as long as you do so within the boundaries of proper grammar and correct spelling).

Essay Questions Are Going To Make You Think

Essay questions vary from one university or college to the next. It is in your best interest to have a few essays of varying subject matter ready just in case you need a generic essay to submit for admission or aid award applications. Below you will find a list of sample essay questions similar to those commonly asked on applications or in interviews by certain university admissions administrators:

- What is your idea of the perfect adventure?
- What do you value the most in relationships? Why do you think that you feel this way?
- You have just finished writing your 300-page autobiography. Please describe page 225.
- Talk about the one person you feel the closest to and tell us what you think makes your bond with this person a strong one.

- If you could declare your own holiday, what would it celebrate? Why? How would you have people observe it?

Honesty Is Still the Best Policy, Honestly

The truth is, if you're a student applicant, you're better off just writing about what you know than you are trying to pass yourself off as a person or personality type that you have never been. "To thine own self be true," wrote Shakespeare. How true his words are. It does you no good to write out a four-page essay on why you chose to be a music major if you honestly do not know these reasons yourself. If you find that you truly don't know the answer to a question, you might write a four-page paper about the reasons for your questions and how you feel that attending this school will help you find the answer to this inner debate.

Stay Ahead of the Game

Don't you hate it when you meet someone who only seems to be trying to impress everyone? Well, admissions officers do too. Don't try to do, say, or write what you think they want to hear. Just be you. Do what you think is right, and say what you believe.

For extra advice or coaching on how to prepare and compose a college admissions essay, think about consulting with your teachers or guidance counselors at your high school. (An English teacher would likely be most helpful, at least as a proofreader.) Go ahead and ask a couple of people to read your essay. Getting more than one opinion will help you edit your work into a more thoughtful and complete submission.

All of this admissions stuff will get you in the door. Along with forms, essays, and interviews, there are fees for applications. Do your research and know what you're getting into. This is just the first step. Once you get in—that's when the real cost challenges arise! But to get to that stage, you need to go through this one. Do it right and you'll be on the road to a bright future!

Chapter 3

SCHOLARSHIPS— SOMETHING FOR EVERYONE!

S cholarships are a good way to ease the financial burden of paying for college. Even if you are thinking "what could I even get a scholarship for?"—it's probably possible! However, you must be ambitious, since it is up to you to seek out and apply for awards. Each scholarship requires applicants to meet certain criteria, applicants should not expect to simply be handed a scholarship. A good deal of work is involved—are you up for the challenge? It could have *major* rewards!

SCHOLARSHIP ELIGIBILITY—SHOW'EM WHAT YOU'RE WORKING WITH!

You should be happily surprised once you start looking for scholarships to qualify for! If you're looking in the right places, you will discover that there are as many types of scholarships as there are types of students! Frequently, a scholarship comes with eligibility requirements that tailor it to students of a particular background. Many scholarships are geared toward an applicant's major, while others reward athletic ability. For some, the applicant's parents determine the student's eligibility (such as scholarships for children of veterans). Still other scholarships are awarded on the basis of a student's social, ethnic, or religious background, such as scholarships from the United Negro College Fund, or on the student's gender or sexual orientation, like those made available only to women or only to transgender students.

Tell Me—What Exactly Is a Scholarship?

The best thing about scholarships is that they are usually awards that do not have to be paid back, given for the purpose of aiding in payment of education costs! Sometimes, scholarship foundations or the individual donors for a scholarship will attach certain requirements that a student must meet to receive and keep the scholarship. If the student fails to fulfill these requirements after the scholarship has been awarded, the money may need to be returned. In some cases, failing to meet requirements may result in the scholarship being reverted into the form of a loan—as Pennsylvania does with its NETS (New Economy Technology Scholarships) program.

Will It Pay for Everything?

Some scholarships are guaranteed for a certain dollar amount, percentage of tuition costs, or to remain in effect for a certain length of time or for a specified number of semesters. Some might even last for the entire duration of a student's enrollment, all the way up to the completion of the bachelor's degree. Some scholarships expire after a certain length of time, but these may also be renewable. If the student applies again at the end of the award term and can provide evidence that all the minimum criteria requirements continue to be met or even exceeded (such as a specified level of athletic performance or a minimum GPA), that student may continue to receive the scholarship for an additional term.

SAVVY STUDENTS SAVE

Scholarship applications often require additional documents, such as a high school transcript, letter of recommendation, an essay, or a copy of the student's federal Student Aid Report (SAR) before the application is considered complete. Review the application requirements carefully, and be sure to include all required supporting documents. If your application is complete, on time, and well constructed, you will probably be a strong candidate!

Other scholarships are exclusively one-time awards. Don't view that as a bad thing—money that pays for your education, even for one semester or one year, is always a good thing; don't turn up your nose at it because it comes in the form of a single lump sum. Scholarships range in value from hundreds of dollars to thousands, and in some cases have been known to pay for an individual's entire tuition bill.

Scholarships Versus Grants? Accept Either One

Try hard not to confuse a scholarship with a grant. Unfortunately, this is a lot easier said than done. The terms "scholarship" and "grant" are sometimes used interchangeably, even by those parties who award them, and this has become the cause for a lot of confusion about the actual differences between the two. More often than not, scholarships are awarded based upon some form of outstanding achievement or something else that makes the student stand apart from others (such as athletic ability, artistic or musical talent, or life experience), whereas most grants are based solely upon a student's financial need. The good news is scholarships and grants usually do not need to be repaid.

MOST COMMON TYPES OF SCHOLARSHIPS

While there are scores of different scholarship types to be found out there, some are more common than others. Roughly speaking, scholarships come in two main categories: those based on merit and those based on need. Merit-based scholarships can be broken down even further into subgroups such as gender-based, academic, musical ability, and athletic.

Stay Ahead of the Game

Institutional scholarships are those that are made available by the college to which students are applying. They can be awarded upon admission or applied for after acceptance and throughout a student's enrollment. Non-institutional scholarships are all other awards that come from outside the college or university.

Gender-Based Scholarships—Male or Female?

Some scholarships are based on an applicant's gender. Don't rule these out as an option—find out what the school you are interested in offers. Athletic scholarship regulations permit Division I and II colleges to offer more male or more female scholarships in different sports, so the chances of being awarded an athletic scholarship for a particular sport might be better for male players, while another sport may offer more scholarships for females. Female students should not overlook schools with more scholarships for males. The scholarships that are awarded to female student-athletes may be substantially larger than those from a school where such scholarships are commonplace.

While some of the more obscure scholarships might not be what you would normally think of as big-dollar financial aid, obtaining even a few of them could add up to significant money. Three $500 scholarships add up to $1,500 and, to most people, that is quite a bit of money. Remember that every dollar you can get in scholarship money is money you don't have to borrow—meaning less money you will have to eventually pay back.

Athletics Versus Academics—
The Battle for Money

Almost all institutions of higher learning have academic scholarship programs. Depending on the scholarship, eligibility is based on a student's high school academic achievement and test scores or on academic excellence as a college student. Schools often have much more flexibility in the way they administer these academic scholarship programs than they do for athletic scholarships. This is because the National Collegiate Athletics Association (NCAA), along with the other athletic conferences, has a laundry list of rules and regulations regarding the award of athletic scholarships. These rules are often based upon what athletic division the school belongs to and in what sport(s) they host teams.

Some sports that fall into NCAA Divisions I and II are restricted in the number of scholarships the institution is allowed to award, whereas NCAA Division III schools are completely forbidden from recognizing athletic ability with scholarships. So, apparently the old myth about how athletics are favored over academics when it comes to scholarships is unfounded—at least at some schools.

Are You Smart, Financially Needy, or Both?

While some scholarships are based on academic, artistic, humanitarian, or athletic merits, others are based solely upon a student's financial need. There are some scholarships, however, that recognize both merit and financial need, so do not rule out anything that you might qualify for.

An example of a scholarship program that recognizes both academics and financial need is the Kansas State Scholarship. Between 1,000 and 1,500 scholarships are given out annually to students who are Kansas residents with a minimum 3.0 GPA who have demonstrated financial need. Applications, FAFSAs, test scores, and transcripts are required of all applicants.

SAVVY STUDENTS SAVE

Always know what the terms and/or limitations of a scholarship are before you apply. Remember, meeting the criteria at application does not guarantee you will be able to meet the ongoing requirements to keep the scholarship.

Many institutions and private sources have scholarships for students with outstanding high school academic records. If there is no mention of the student's or parents' income or asset information on the application materials, you can assume that financial need is not among the criteria.

WELCOME TO THE JUNGLE!— YOU ANIMAL ENOUGH TO WIN THE FIGHT FOR FUNDS?

Yes, it is a cliché, but it's true—it is a jungle out there! Looking for the right scholarship can make anyone start to feel a little bit overwhelmed. How are you supposed to decide which scholarships to apply for? How do you know if you have a better chance of getting one than another?

Well, the first thing anyone who plans to find a scholarship needs to do is to make out a list of "possibles." This means making a list of all scholarships that you are qualified to receive. You might not necessarily be applying for all of them, so feel free to make this list as long as you can.

47

SCHOLARSHIPS—SOMETHING FOR EVERYONE!

As you know, some scholarships are based on merit, others on need, and some recognize both. Do not rule out anything that you even remotely qualify for. Financial need, especially, is defined by different standards by different scholarship donors. Some might base their evaluation upon demonstrated financial need as determined by the government through the FAFSA (Free Application for Federal Student Aid). Other scholarship committees might consider you "needy" just because you do not already have enough scholarships and/or grant money to cover the cost of your education.

Stay Ahead of the Game

When searching for scholarship opportunities, do not apply for scholarships that require you to choose a major you are not interested in. It's a bad idea to choose educational goals and a career path that are not a good fit for you, no matter how much money the scholarship is worth.

Rather than ruling something out because you aren't positive you qualify, take a chance and fill it out. It only takes a little time (relatively speaking) to fill out a scholarship application. Think about it this way. Let's say it takes you four hours to complete an application for something as small as a $100 scholarship. If you get it, that's the equivalent of $25 an hour for your work—pretty good money for a high school student who gets $6 an hour to clean out grease vats at the local fast-food joint.

Where to Find Scholarships?

As mentioned earlier, students and parents should think of themselves as private investigators when searching for scholarship opportunities. Don't leave any stone unturned when it comes to finding awards that you might qualify for. Ask at each school you are interested in. Do a little Internet surfing. Sign up for a free membership with a few scholarship-savvy Web sites that have good search engines for scholarships, such as *www.fastweb.com*, *www.petersons.com*, or *www.collegeboard.com*. Keep a sharp eye on the local newspaper. Check with various state and federal agencies. If nothing else—ask around!

Your New Best Friend: Your High School Guidance Counselor

It is a guidance counselor's job to help students with matters concerning what they plan to do after graduation. Therefore, scholarships should be among any guidance counselor's specialties. Make it a point to apply for any scholarships that you can find through your guidance counselor, as these are often focused specifically toward high school students.

Few guidance counselors have the time to hunt down individual students to tell them when a new scholarship opportunity becomes available. However, if they have seen your face often enough to be able to put your name with it, they just might hunt you down. It is up to you as a student to stay on top of what scholarships are available throughout your senior year.

SAVVY STUDENTS SAVE

You live in a world that now has the Internet. So, for goodness sakes, use it! Among the information available is a seemingly endless number of scholarships. Some scholarships even have online applications. You can apply for these with nothing more than a short e-mail essay.

Look Right Under Your Nose!

Check in the local community as well. Some local health-care agencies, for instance, offer scholarships to college students who plan to study nursing. In return, the student agrees to a work obligation for a certain period of time, either during or after the educational program.

There are also service organizations, such as parent-teacher organizations, athletic associations, the Elks Club, Kiwanis, Lions Club, and so on, that may offer scholarships for deserving students in the surrounding community. Keep an eye on the local newspaper for possible scholarship information.

Some scholarship foundations designate banks to manage scholarship funds. You or your parents might want to contact some of the local nonprofit organizations or even their bank representatives to inquire about possible scholarships.

YOU *WILL* QUALIFY FOR SOMETHING

If someone says that they were unable to get a scholarship because they did not qualify for any, they are not being truthful to you (or to themselves, most likely). The same goes for applications. "There aren't any scholarships that I qualify to even apply for," is about as true as saying, "I don't have anything to wear." Neither of these statements is true. There is always something to wear; you just do not want to wear what you have. In the same way, there are always scholarships you qualify for; you just need to be willing to do the work.

A School's Scholarship Program Isn't One Size Fits All

All colleges are different, and their scholarship programs are just as different from one school to the next. One institution might offer only a handful of scholarships to its best-qualified applicants, while another institution may have the funds to offer several hundred separate scholarships. A student might get a full-tuition scholarship at one college and not be awarded as much as a dime at another. If you haven't made a final decision yet on which college or university to attend, don't rule out the idea of checking with the financial aid departments of several schools. See what kind of scholarships they offer and whether they fit you. Just because you're not eligible for any scholarships at one school doesn't mean you won't find the perfect fit at the next.

Persistence Can Pay the Bills!

It is not enough to do one simple Internet search before you decide to give up. If you have trouble finding enough possible scholarships after one search, modify your search terms and try again. Don't forget to keep checking your state's higher education assistance agency. There may be financial aid grants and scholarships available for residents of your state that may even be transferable if you attend an out-of-state institution.

Scholarship opportunities are available to students from a variety of sources—the federal government, colleges to which a student is applying, private scholarship donors, businesses, nonprofit organizations, and philanthropic foundations. Some of the Greek social organizations (fraternities and sororities) and honor societies offer scholarships. Investigate possible opportunities in these areas if you are a member. Check out both local and national scholarship possibilities. Be sure you understand that at this point, these are nothing more than opportunities. Scholarships do not just come to you, and application is not a guarantee of an award.

CAN PARENTS APPLY?

Sometimes, when trying to get a scholarship, *what* you know is not nearly as important as *who* you know. Other times, it's even more important to figure out who your parents know—more specifically, where your parents work and what they have done in their lives. Does this mean that parents should try to use their personal influences to squeeze out scholarship money for their kids? Not necessarily—in fact, many parents simply don't need to.

Go After that Employee Scholarship

If you are a parent, your place of employment may offer scholarships or grants to your children simply because you are an employee. If you are a prospective student, you might want to ask your parents about checking to see whether their employers sponsor such programs.

For example, United Technologies Corporation (or UTC, owner of aerodynamics manufacturing giant Pratt & Whitney) has established a scholarship program meant to assist the children of employees planning to pursue higher education at a college or university. These renewable scholarships are offered in the amount of $3,000 each year and are awarded for the term of that year for full-time study at an accredited four-year college or university of the student's choice.

These awards are given for undergraduate study only, and renewal is limited to no more than three additional years (for a total of four years) or until the student has completed a bachelor's degree—whichever happens first. Renewal is decided based upon whether the student displays satisfactory academic performance in a full-time course of study and whether UTC continues the program.

SAVVY STUDENTS SAVE

Although many employers now offer college scholarships or even full tuition grants for the children or dependents of employees, be sure you check the fine print. Most of the time, the employee must be active and working full-time, and the student dependent must attend a four-year study program at an accredited university to receive the award.

Even if you are not an employee of the abovementioned company, your employer may have a similar program. For instance, GTE hosts a similar program. There are even scholarships available to the children of public school employees. Remember that it never hurts to ask about scholarships, and you cannot know if they exist without asking. Parents should contact their employers' human resources departments to find out if they host such a program. If so, schedule an appointment with a representative or request materials that include any further details.

Children of Veterans Scholarships

More scholarships are available to the children of veterans than you can shake a stick at. Some universities, such as the University of Illinois, actually host Children of Veterans scholarship programs—with scholarship money specifically set aside for the children of military veterans.

There is also a Children of Vietnam Veterans Scholarship fund, with a collective total of $100,000 in scholarships awarded each year. The American Legion Auxiliary National President's Scholarship is also awarded solely to the children of veterans who served in the U.S. Armed Forces, as are the Amvets' Scholarships.

Stay Ahead of the Game!

If you are a dependent (that is, a child or a spouse) of an active duty member of any branch of the U.S. Armed Forces, the federal government will pay for as much as 75 percent of your tuition costs.

YOU GET ONE SHOT AT EACH APPLICATION, SO MAKE IT A GOOD ONE

No two scholarship applications are identical. The work that you have to put in to complete those applications is as diverse as the scholarships available. At the scholarship-savvy FastWeb site, for example (*www.fast-web.com*), students can register their unique student profile free of charge and find information on hundreds of scholarships, internships, and grants. The profile asks questions that, once submitted, are compared with the criteria for thousands of scholarships. Those that come back as matches are then compiled and listed on the student's account. However, because many scholarships have multiple eligibility requirements, you will not qualify for all the matches that your search returns. It will take a lot of time and perseverance, whether you work online or by more old-fashioned methods (such as the library), to find scholarships that are completely suited to your needs. Once you find those scholarships that do match your qualifications, fill out each form completely, modifying your information to fit the questions on each unique application. You want each completed form to look like you took your time and completed it conscientiously!

Put the Time In!

Students and parents should expect to spend a certain amount of time and effort searching out and applying for scholarships. As a student, you must also understand that there is a good possibility that you will have to write a different essay every time you apply for a new scholarship. Yes, it's more work than you may have planned for, but hey, if it means getting to go to the college of your dreams isn't it worth it?

Be sure to make copies of all your scholarship applications, as well as your scholarship essays, and keep them in a folder. Sometimes you can modify these essays and applications and make them work for more than just one scholarship application.

What Makes You Eligible?

As you begin to search through scholarship application forms, you may find some with long or detailed lists of eligibility requirements. Do not let the detailed criteria of a scholarship discourage you; instead, fill out an application for anything that remotely seems to fit you or your student. Even if a scholarship application lists both merit- and need-based criteria, the selection committee might weigh one factor much more heavily than the other. A scholarship applicant who is not exactly stellar academically (meaning a GPA of less than the almighty 4.0) with verifiable financial need might be awarded a scholarship over a much more academically qualified applicant with less financial need, or vice versa. Applying for scholarships doesn't cost you anything, so if you think it's possible you might be considered, send in an application. You have nothing to lose and only money to gain.

Chapter 4

HANDLING THE COSTS

W here should you draw the line financially? Your financial boundaries are yours and yours alone. Sure you can commiserate with fellow students or parents about the ever-rising costs, but your family's reality is unlike any others! Here, you will find an explanation of what these boundaries are, how to identify them, and most importantly how to stay inside them. But that's not the end of the line—once you know your current financial boundaries, you have to decide whether you want to remain within their limits or whether you are willing to stretch a little and invest more in your future. Got you thinking yet?

UNDERSTANDING FINANCIAL BOUNDARIES

The process of understanding your financial boundaries involves three essential steps: figuring out what financial boundaries actually are (and what they are not), learning how to identify your own, and knowing how to stay within them. Let's start with step one.

As a parent, especially, it is important that you understand your financial boundaries. If you know what you can afford, you and your student will be able to choose a school realistically as soon as you receive the financial aid packages and calculate the net cost to you. Everyone will only become frustrated if you don't realize your boundaries until after the student has committed to attend a certain college. What will you do when your student gains admission and pays a deposit only to find that you are uninformed or unprepared to make up for the costs that are outside your immediate financial boundaries?

CHEAP$KATE

Don't rule out applying to certain schools just because of their total cost of attendance! Even students and parents of very modest financial means can afford costly Ivy League institutions if they receive enough financial aid! However, you need to be prepared and in order to do this, you must understand financial boundaries.

Financial boundaries are not meant to discourage you or to sway your confidence in your ability to pay for a college education. This is simply a way for you to get a ballpark idea of what you have as a base for paying for college. Knowing your boundaries gives you a chance to take a hard, realistic look at your financial situation so you can figure out what you need in order to fund your journey to a higher education.

What Are Financial Boundaries?

Roughly speaking, financial boundaries are the limits of your finances. They give you a clear understanding of what you can and cannot afford. This information can help you plan ahead, allowing you to determine your needs by defining what you already have. This is also a good way to get an early heads-up about whether you need or qualify for certain kinds of financial aid. If you are taking out loans to help pay for college, just determine how much you can afford to pay monthly now (if a parent loan) or after graduation (if a student loan) and stay within those projected limits.

SAVVY STUDENTS SAVE

Communication and asking questions is key! Students and parents should discuss the kinds of financial aid the student is eligible for, know the source of each type of aid, and understand any obligations associated with that assistance.

Can Boundaries Keep You from College?

Going to college should never be a matter of "if." Decide, right from the start, that you *are* going to go to college. Keep this in mind throughout the process. It will happen! Questions are fine, but instead of "Am I going?" the questions you should ask are "How much?" "When?" "What kind?" and "Where?" In other words, spend time thinking about:

- *How much* money do you and your family have, in savings or otherwise?
- *When* do you expect to have more?
- *What kind* of school do you wish to attend?
- *Where* in the family, or elsewhere, can you go for help? (This includes loans and other financial aid.)

CHEAP$KATE

Decide now what you are willing to borrow each year for education purposes and stick to it. Sacrifice in other areas so you can put all of your resources into your education investment.

GIVE THOSE BOUNDARIES A BOOST

Financial boundaries are not to be feared, and they should never be perceived as a curse. These boundaries do not condemn you, nor do they confine you in any way, shape, or form. In fact, there are a number of ways to improve or expand the abilities and limits of your financial boundaries. Staying positive is crucial, and the following tips may be just what you need to help you get started making your financial picture better than it ever has been.

One Thing about Debt—Keep It Under Control!

Excessive debt? What does that mean really? Well, just ask a majority of the American population! In the United States, debt continues to rise among the average citizen while the amount and frequency of our individual savings have plummeted to a frighteningly low level. We live in a world of immediate gratification, where a plastic card can seemingly give us anything we want, when we want it, without seeing any "actual" money leave our hands.

Trim the Fat!

Borrowing money to help pay for education can be a great investment, but borrow only what is necessary. Reduce the money your family spends on entertainment and other variable expenses by looking for low to no cost alternatives. For example, suppose your family traditionally enjoys a weekend movie night. Don't assume you always have to show up at the theater as the sun sets on a Friday or Saturday. There are several other options to consider. For instance, you could do any of the following:

- See a matinee instead of an evening show.
- Go to the dollar theater and see a second-run movie.
- Rent a movie from the video store.
- Check out a movie from your local library.

Saving on seemingly little expenses like this will really make a difference after a while. Your family's lifestyle might have to change a bit but think of the goal!

You don't have to stop having fun; you just need to start thinking—before you do things—about how much money your fun is costing you. Consider cheaper methods of entertainment whenever you can, and eventually you will see significant changes in the tightness of those financial boundaries. Reducing your family's expenses may mean making a few temporary sacrifices to your customary lifestyle or luxuries. However, in the long run you will find that the reward of providing for your college education was well worth the sacrifice.

Here are a few more suggestions for trimming your expenses as much as possible:

- Read magazines at the library instead of subscribing.
- Find car and home insurance with lower premiums/rates.
- Cut down your cable/satellite bill by switching to a smaller plan.
- Learn to do minor home repairs (within reason) instead of hiring pros.

Another thing to watch out for is excessive cell phone usage. Cell phones and those "out-of-plan" minutes are becoming a notorious means of eating up a family's hard-earned money. Keep tabs on all the minutes each member of your family uses—including yourself. Talk too much, or use too many of those newfangled download options (ring tones are especially popular among today's teens) and you'll find yourself with some high, and often very unexpected, expenses when the bill arrives in the mail. It's definitely in your best interest to stay within the allotted minutes on your wireless plan. With most plans, you can check how many minutes you have used and other important information online. Remember what was said before? Information is free! Why in the world wouldn't you use it to your advantage?

For you homeowners (especially you parents) out there, refinancing your mortgage might be a good way to help expand your financial boundaries. If you can get a significantly lower interest rate, you can open up more available funds to pay for your student's higher education. This is a very valid idea, especially since you get federal tax benefits associated with a mortgage.

Stay Ahead of the Game

If it's just too difficult to stick to your current cell phone plan, it might be wise to consider upgrading so that your bill never exceeds your base monthly charge. A new, bigger plan may only cost you an extra $50 or so a month. However, if every member of your family consistently runs up extra minutes, you're probably already paying hundreds more.

WHAT *IS* TUITION?— MYTH AND REALITY

Everyone knows what tuition is, kind of. However, for someone who has never actually paid it, such as a first-generation college student or a parent whose own college years were funded by a parent or relative, the tuition payment process needs a little explanation. The good news is that tuition payments are a lot more flexible than many people think, and schools are becoming more and more lenient about how and when tuition must be paid.

Many myths surround the process of paying tuition, especially concerning when and how this should happen. Some say it must be paid in full before classes start, while others claim that a student cannot register for classes until all money owed to the school has been paid. According to still other sources, a student will be taken off the roll immediately if the tuition has not been paid. It's a good idea to take a look at these points and figure out what's true and what's not so you know what enrollment issues you could face, especially if you are concerned about your ability to pay on time. Don't get behind on payments or in trouble with tuition just because *you didn't know the rules*!

SAVVY STUDENTS SAVE

Most institutions offer a payment plan that lets you divide tuition for the whole academic year into monthly payments. This makes the cost to families much more manageable. Schools usually don't charge any interest, but you might be assessed a minimal service charge.

What If I'm in Need of Help?

If you take a look at most schools' formal policies, they state that a student's tuition payments must be current in order for the student to attend class. However, this policy often revolves around a loophole. As long as the school receives payment of some kind, it is inconsequential whether the student has actually paid a single dime out of pocket. Loans, even emergency loans, count as forms of tuition payment.

Some colleges now have what they call "emergency" semester loans, which are granted to any student for a single term of attendance. This loan takes the lump sum of the semester's tuition and breaks it down into smaller increments that can be paid out over a period of time. Commonly, there are three pay increments. In other words, if your tuition for a semester is $3,000, you will make three payments of approximately $1,000 over the span of the semester. That's one way of getting the bill paid so you can go to class. Just make sure you pay off the loan as soon as you can afford to do so.

Is a Missed Payment Grounds for Dismissal?

No. These emergency loans may be broken up into increments, but the school does not usually resort to drastic measures if the full portion is not paid by the deadline. Consider the following true example of how tuition payments can work.

A certain student has a total semester tuition cost of $3,000. He pays with an emergency loan, broken up into three $1,000 increments. These payments are due within the first three months of the semester. However, this student also served in the military, and under the GI Bill he is entitled to a $1,200 check after each month of completed and verified full-time college attendance. Now, let's say that our student uses half of the $1,200 to pay his tuition, with the other half going to cover living expenses as well as the cost of textbooks and course supplies. Instead of $1,000, the amount of his incremental payment, the student only has $600 to put toward his tuition. However, he pays that $600 every month. Aside from the occasional late charge, the school business office does not even bat an eye. As long as a school is receiving some payment, they often let something as small as incomplete payments slide by.

It's best not to assume that this example will also hold true at your school. If you're having a problem making your tuition payments on time or in full, you should contact the business office and discuss your options. Ask whether partial payments, such as those in the above example, are a possibility. The simple act of going to the business office to discuss your problem—along with your assurance that you fully intend (and will be able) to pay your tuition—can be enough to open some doors. On the other hand, if they do not hear from you, the school's business office has little choice but to assume the worst. Help them out by going to them and discussing your situation face-to-face.

CHEAP$KATE

Just because a school is lenient about enforcing its payment deadlines, you should not assume that it ignores them completely. Schools will issue fines and late charges. If you can pay on time, do so. If not, take the fine, and pay when you can. Just remember that you need to keep the balance of your account low enough so that your school won't put a hold on it, which can prevent you from registering or receiving a report card.

If Next Semester Isn't Paid Up, Can I Register?

There is leeway on registration up to a certain point. Most schools will allow students to register for classes as long as their balance does not exceed a certain amount. At Midwestern State University, for example, a student who owes the school less than $500 is still allowed to register for the next semester. However, if the student's account goes above the $500 ceiling, a "freeze" or "hold" is placed on the account. This prevents the student from registering, receiving certain honors or awards, and sometimes from receiving a report card or even graduating.

Even though there is some flexibility when it comes to when and how you pay that tuition bill, the fact remains that it must be paid. If you find yourself struggling to make those payments, be sure that you do pay what you are able. Also be sure that you keep your account current (and out of delinquent status) by bringing your balance down under your school's "tuition owed" ceiling before the semester's end.

Stay Ahead of the Game

A "freeze" or "hold" can put a real damper on the close of your semester, especially if it keeps you from registering early for the next semester's classes, receiving a student honor that you were eligible for, or even from getting your grades at term's end.

GRANTS ARE FREE

You remember one thing about grants from the scholarship chapter, don't you? They don't have to be paid back! But different people think of different things when they think of grants, which is understandable because of the lack of a precise definition and the fact that grants can be for any amount of money. Grants can be awarded to you from the federal government, your state government, the college or university that you attend, or from a number of alternative private sources.

Mixing and Matching Terms

Remember that some people use the terms "scholarships" and "grants" interchangeably, as though they were the same thing. It is a good idea to keep this in mind so that you do not overlook an opportunity simply because of what the source of aid is called. For example, maybe you can't demonstrate much financial need because the expected family contribution results on your FAFSA are too high, and you don't think you're eligible to receive any grants. Suppose, then, that an engineering company offers a grant that helps toward tuition costs for any student who majors in engineering. The application for such a grant might require the student to list engineering courses that he or she has taken to the present date along with an explanation of future plans and goals. The company might not even mention (or even consider) financial need in application screenings. (This sounds a lot like a scholarship, doesn't it?) If you had overlooked this because it was called a grant, you could have missed out on extra funding for your college career.

SAVVY STUDENTS SAVE

Each institution has its own particular timeline for notifying recipients of grant awards. The sooner you have completed and filed the FAFSA application, the sooner you are likely to see the results from colleges and universities. Some institutions will even do the estimates for your financial aid package early if you are willing to complete a special form or if you are considered a serious prospective student of that institution.

They're Both Good—So Lump Them Together

It doesn't matter whether the money you apply for is called a "scholarship," a "grant," or an "award." All of these terms are considered "grant assistance" in the financial aid field. Let's face it. If someone wants to give you money to help pay for your education, do you really care what they call it? The truth is that scholarships and grants are equal—neither is really better than the other. Obviously, grants *are* better than taking out loans or getting an extra job. Find out which ones you qualify for, and apply for them!

SEARCH FOR "FREE MONEY"

"Free money" does not mean money that magically rains down from the sky and lands in your lap like a gift from the heavens as you drive off to college. The "free" part of free money means that this is money you do not have to pay back to anyone, ever. That is undoubtedly the best part about free money—no interest, no regret, and no financial backfiring.

Unfortunately, prospective college students often make the mistake of thinking that just because the money is free, it will be easier to get and all they have to do is apply for it. In fact, getting these funds may not be as easy as you think. Students who want to receive the benefits of free-and-clear financial aid will have to do a lot of work and searching to locate and be granted any form of free money.

CHEAP$KATE

Even finding a source of free money doesn't guarantee that you will get it—you still may have to fulfill obligations such as grades, volunteerism, or participation in certain activities. Once you find something you qualify for, you still have to apply and be accepted.

Find This So-Called "Free Money"

You've already learned a great deal about scholarships and grants. Free money usually comes in one of these two forms; however, you might also find it under another name, such as a reduction, rebate, or waiver of an educational expense that you otherwise would have had to pay.

Working hard at getting good grades in high school and getting involved in activities is likely to help you receive all the free money you will need to pay your way at some colleges, but *only* if you are extremely diligent in searching for it. While researching and visiting the different colleges and universities you are interested in, you and your parents should make it a point to find out exactly what kind of and how many scholarships or other opportunities are available, what amounts they are available in, and how and when to apply for them.

A financial aid administrator can assist families in applying for federal, state, and institutional aid, but don't make the mistake of stopping your search for free money there. Internet searches can be another good way for parents and students to locate payback-free money. Do searches for grants and scholarships on different search engines.

CHEAP$KATE

Sign up for scholarship searches, but avoid those that require a fee for the service. Some well-known and reputable scholarship search Web sites are: *www.fastweb.com, www.srnexpress.com, www.collegenet.com,* and *www .collegeboard.com* (through the "For Students" link).

Of course, private sources of aid may also be available to students through their high school, community, or local businesses. These unique opportunities can be found in your particular geographic area, and they are not usually advertised nationally. Keep your eyes and ears open for any advertisements or notices of local financial aid resources that may be available only in your area. Programs offered by your state are another possible source of free grant or scholarship assistance.

How Do I Get Free Money?

At some colleges, all you need to do to be considered for scholarship awards is simply complete the application for admission. At other schools, however, more may be required—such as multiple applications, additional information, or essays. Students and parents should do their best to find out what kind of aid is offered at a school, what is required to get it, and when pertinent information is required. Be sure that grant and scholarship deadlines are not missed. Few donors of student financial aid are even willing to accept late applications, and if they do accept them, applicant tardiness is sometimes marked on the application.

SAVVY STUDENTS SAVE

Impressions matter! When you tour colleges and attend campus visit days, you are not only *getting* an impression of the college, you are *giving* an impression too. Don't act immature. Some of the people you meet may sit on scholarship committees and remember how you acted.

CONSIDER YOUR *SEAT*

Some students are pretty successful at searching for scholarships, grants, and other free-money opportunities on the Internet. Others, however, spend hours upon hours searching and applying just to get a whole lot of nothing in return. How can some students generate cash for college so easily while others just end up wasting their time? The answer is simple—they know how to use a SEAT. This handy little acronym refers to the four basic elements to a successful pursuit of free money for college—"Scores, Effort, Appearance, and Timing."

Scores Equal Credentials

As if the SATs aren't stressful enough, let's add this tip—a student who scores high on the SATs certainly has a better chance at winning a scholarship than a student who scored half that does. The higher your scores, the more scholarship and grant opportunities you are eligible to apply for. You can visualize your financial-aid opportunities as an upside-down pyramid—the higher you get, the more money is available. Your good grades and test scores will move you up toward this wider range of aid possibilities. For example, scholarships may be allotted for students who are in the top 5 percent of their high school graduating class, with SAT scores of at least 1300 (on the verbal and math sections) and a minimum grade point average of 3.6 or higher on a 4.0 scale. A student with strong academic credentials will likely be eligible for scholarships like these, while a student with poorer scores will have fewer options to choose from. Some institutions will also consider the new writing portion of the SAT when awarding scholarships, other schools still use only the verbal and math sections.

Keep in mind that even if you are a higher-scoring student, if you fail to get your application in the mail on time, or choose not to make the effort, someone who is better organized and more ambitious might get in instead (despite their lower scores).

E is for Effort

If you are not exactly a high-scoring test taker, this is not a reason for panic. There are plenty of other kinds of free money that are not based solely upon a student's academic merit. Maybe you didn't get the most stellar score on the SAT. You will still find opportunities to qualify for free money. For instance, some programs are based on non-scholastic factors such as gender, race, ethnicity, financial need, hobbies, volunteerism, special needs, or a parent's vocation or employer. Your credentials and background might help you qualify for free money that is unavailable to a so-called "smarter" student. You just need to put in the time and effort to find these opportunities and take advantage of them.

CHEAP$KATE

Look in the most logical place! You can save yourself a lot of time and learn a lot by reviewing each school's financial aid section of their web site. Pick up the phone and call or send an e-mail if you want more information or have questions about an institution's scholarships or grants.

Don't fool yourself by thinking that just because you took several hours to search and apply for a couple of free money opportunities, you are a shoe-in to get at least one of them. Success is going to take a *lot* of effort. Applying for free money is a lot like applying for a job—sometimes it takes quite a few tries before you get a positive response.

SAVVY STUDENTS SAVE

Your search for free money can fit into three categories: government aid, institutional aid, and aid from other sources. Take the initiative in all three areas. Work with an institution's financial aid office to apply for all the government and institutional aid you possibly can. Use some private-investigator skills, the Internet, or even old-fashioned resources like your local public library to find financial aid from all other sources.

Try to complete as much of your search as possible before you graduate from high school (if that's still possible). No matter how much searching you did in high school, however, you should continue this search throughout college. New opportunities become available all the time, and you do not want to miss out on them. Understand that you are going to have to set aside time to put some *effort* into this. Just think of the Internet search for free money as good practice for all of the research and writing that you will have to do when college time finally arrives.

It's especially important that you keep track of your efforts, what sites you visit, and what scholarships you apply for. By staying organized, you will not waste time duplicating your work unnecessarily by applying to schol-

MR. CHEAP'S GUIDE TO PAYING FOR COLLEGE

arships multiple times just because you forgot which ones you already applied for. You might even be able to modify one essay to fit another application—if you were organized enough to save the original essays and can remember what you named the file (or where you hid the hard copies).

Appearance—First Impressions Don't Happen Twice

It is not just what you say that matters but how you say it. Although it is possible to be a bit too boastful, a student has more to fear from being too modest when filling out applications for free money. Administrators may have to read through hundreds, even thousands, of applications before deciding on who is awarded funding. You want your application to be more than a fair and honest presentation of who you are and what you're about—you also want it to stand apart from everyone else's application.

Timing Is Everything So Start Now

Some students wait until after they graduate from high school to begin searching for free money. High school seniors are so busy with all kinds of time-consuming things like homework, school activities, applying to colleges, and the myriad social activities that take place during the year. College is an entire year away, after all, and it just does not seem reasonable to get all stressed out about money so far in advance.

These students plan to wait until they have a little more free time and all their high school activities are finally over. The bad news is that by that time, most opportunities for free money have already passed them by. That's because deadlines and application due dates fall at some point during the year prior to when the student will begin college—in other words, the student's senior year of high school. This means that by the time he or she graduates from high school, the deadline for application is already long passed.

How do you avoid this situation? The ideal mode of action is to start investigating scholarship opportunities in the student's junior year of high school (even freshman and sophomore years are not too early). This way, you already know the deadline dates in advance and can mark them down on your senior timeline (whatever that is). You might even be able to do some of the more time-consuming work in advance (such as writing essays).

CHEAP$KATE

In some instances, your search for free money can include a waiver of the admissions application fee. Many institutions offer an application fee waiver if you apply for admission by a certain date, attend certain campus visit programs, or schedule an on-campus interview and tour.

Remember, free money is not just outside scholarship money. It's any money you don't have to pay. Grant money is free money, too. Students and parents should make sure to complete the FAFSA by the earliest required deadline and complete any additional forms that are needed before the deadline. You could needlessly miss out on a lot of free money opportunities if you miss a deadline due to bad timing. So get started!

Chapter 5

FIGURE IT OUT: FAFSA AND FINANCIAL AID— YOU CAN'T HAVE ONE WITHOUT THE OTHER

Some type of financial aid is always available to those who want or need it. However, the amount of aid you receive (and whether you end up getting any at all) depends on how much paperwork you are willing to sort through, how well you understand the requirements, and if you can meet the deadlines. The best way to avoid hassles is to know exactly what information you need and have it readily accessible.

THE INS AND OUTS OF
THE FAFSA PROCESS

The acronym FAFSA stands for "Free Application for Federal Student Aid." What exactly is a FAFSA? It sounds like the name for some new cola. No, friends, the FAFSA is not quite so tasty. In fact, the FAFSA process can be downright infuriating, pushing some to the edge of a mental breakdown. If you're applying for any type of aid, chances are you'll get to know this form well—most colleges and universities require that all students applying for any kind of aid complete it each year.

How Does the FAFSA Work?

The information you put on the FAFSA is entered into a formula called the Federal Need Analysis Methodology (or just "federal methodology" for short), which measures the financial strength of your family unit. Although the general aspects of the need analysis formula remain the same for many years, there are annual updates, similar to those in the IRS tax code, that result in slight changes each year. Every once in a while Congress will make more significant changes to laws that affect the FAFSA and other aspects of student financial aid. The Higher Education Reconciliation Act (HERA), Public Law 109-171, is part of the Deficit Reduction Act. It was approved by the Senate on December 21, 2005, approved by the House on February 2, 2006, and signed into law by the President on February 8, 2006. The HERA resulted in some changes to the federal methodology calculation.

There are actually three different formulas. One is for dependent students, and two are for independent students (one for students with dependents other than a spouse, and another for students who have no dependents other than a spouse). The central processing system (CPS) uses these formulas to calculate what is called an "expected family contribution" (or EFC) for each applicant. This is the amount of money that the federal government determines your family should pay toward your education.

SAVVY STUDENTS SAVE

Applicants should never use someone else's information when filling out the FAFSA. Each individual student is required to complete his or her own application. Failure to do so could result in the denial, reduction, or revocation of benefits.

The Expected Family Contribution (EFC)

An applicant's expected family contribution, or EFC, is a determination, made with the federal methodology, of the amount of money that the family unit should be expected to contribute toward the higher education of the student. It is not necessarily what you *will* pay. Rather, this expected amount gives financial aid administrators a figure to work with when determining your aid. You may actually end up paying more or less than the calculated EFC.

This EFC formula has two parts: the parents' portion and the student's portion. Each portion is based on a formula that includes both the family members' continuous income from the prior calendar year as well as their owned assets. Parents and students simply enter their information onto the form, submit it, and the formula automatically calculates the student's EFC.

The EFC for two college students who are in the same family will most likely be slightly different because the student portion will be unique for each of them as individual applicants. It is highly unlikely that both students would end up with exactly the same income and assets.

The Parent Portion

The parent portion of the EFC is based on the parents' adjusted available income, which is a combination of available income and a portion of the parents' assets. First, the formula takes the parents' available income listed on the FAFSA (both taxed and untaxed income) and subtracts certain allowances for nondiscretionary expenses (such as taxes and minimal living expenses). The amount that is subtracted from available income is determined according to a special table in the formula that considers the number of parents and college students in the household.

SAVVY STUDENTS SAVE

On the FAFSA, investments do not include your principal place of residence, the value of life insurance policies, retirement plans, prepaid tuition plans, and cash, savings, and checking account balances are reported in other questions.

Next, the parents' assets are considered. Not all assets are counted in determining the adjusted available income. A portion is protected based on the age of the older parent, according to another table in the formula. The federal methodology for the academic year 2007–2008 dictates that remaining assets be multiplied by 12 percent. Once the available income and assets contribution are calculated and added together to get the adjusted available income, a formula is used to determine the parent portion of the expected family contribution.

The Student Portion

The student's portion of the FAFSA, though oftentimes lower, is of substantial importance. The student's available income is determined by taking his or her total income (again, both taxed and untaxed), and then subtracting certain allowances. Some of the income protection allowances for figuring out the student's portion are different than those that are made for the parents.

For example, in the 2007–2008 calculation, the first $3,000 of a student applicant's income is protected. This means that anything a student earns up to that amount is not counted toward the expected family contribution. Also different is the fact that, unlike the contribution calculation for the parents' portion, there is absolutely no protection for a student applicant's assets. All of a student applicant's total assets (meaning cash, savings and checking account balances, investments, and business net worth that are not part of the student's occupational/regular income) are counted at 20 percent.

CHEAP$KATE

Do not forget to count as untaxed income any payments you made to tax-deferred pension and savings plans, whether paid directly or withheld from your earnings. These are usually reported in box 12 of W-2 tax forms with codes D, E, F, G, H, and S. Untaxed contributions to IRA, SEP, SIMPLE, and Keogh accounts also count as untaxed income.

Once the parents' portion and the student's portion of the EFC are determined, they are added together to get the total EFC for the student's upcoming academic year. That amount will be the same regardless of what institution the student decides to attend. However, you should remember that your FAFSA total does not necessarily determine exactly what you end up paying toward your tuition.

Two Big Ways to Save

There are two shortened versions of the FAFSA calculation, the Simplified EFC Formula and the Automatic Zero EFC Calculation, for families in certain situations. Students may have their EFCs calculated for 2007–2008 by the Simplified EFC Formula in which assets are not considered in their calculation if the following conditions are met:

- Anyone included in the parents' household (or student's household, if independent) received benefits during the base year from any of these designated means-tested Federal benefit programs:

  Supplemental Security Income (SSI) Program, which includes:
    ▸ the Food Stamp Program
    ▸ the Free and Reduced Price School Lunch Program
    ▸ the Temporary Assistance for Needy Families (TANF) program
    ▸ the Special Supplemental Nutrition Program for Women, Infants, and Children (WIC)

OR

- the student's parents (or student and spouse, if independent) filed or are eligible to file a 2006 IRS Form 1040A or 1040 EZ (not required to file Form 1040) or are not required to file any federal income tax return

AND

- the 2006 income of the student's parents' (or student and spouse, if independent) adjusted gross income (or total of W-2 earnings, if non-filer) is less than $50,000.

Even better than not having assets counted is an automatic zero EFC! For the 2007–2008 academic year, students who meet the above requirements, but have a total household income level of $20,000 or less can automatically qualify for an EFC of zero. That doesn't necessarily mean you won't have to pay anything for college, but it does mean that you should qualify for a *lot* more aid.

SAVVY STUDENTS SAVE

In order to qualify for the Simplified EFC Formula or an Automatic Zero EFC Formula, you must answer the relevant questions on the FAFSA correctly.

FILLING OUT THE FORMS

You can either complete the FAFSA on paper (and send it in by mail), or you can speed things up by filling it out online. The online application is often a much better option than dealing with the paper version. Both you and the schools that you list on the form will receive your results much sooner, and there is also a greatly reduced chance for making errors.

Regardless of the method you use, paper or electronic, both the student and one parent must sign the form. Obviously, if you complete the paper version, you can sign with a good old blue or black pen. If you use the online version, you have a couple of different options for signing the form. You can print the signature page, sign it in pen, and mail it in (again, mail slows the process), or you can sign electronically, using a personal identification number (PIN).

Getting a PIN and doing the online FAFSA is a good idea. Not only does it speed up your FAFSA results, but you can also use your PIN for other important things, such as accessing the National Student Loan Data System to view a history of your student loans. If you end up attending a college or university that participates in the direct loan program, then you can use your PIN to access your direct loan account information, and to e-sign your master promissory note. Getting a PIN is quick and easy. Just apply on the Web site (*www.FAFSA.ed.gov*) and wait three days. You will receive an e-mail telling you how to retrieve your PIN electronically, or you can elect to wait seven to ten days and receive the PIN in the mail.

Stay Ahead of the Game

Don't forget your PIN! Keep your PIN in a safe place so you can use it for other things in addition to signing the FAFSA. You can use your PIN to view the status of a submitted FAFSA application, to print a copy of your SAR, and to access your Federal Student Aid information on the National Student Loan Data System (NSLDS) Web site.

FAFSA Deadlines—Meet Them or Miss Out

The federal deadline for filing the FAFSA isn't until June 30 of the year *after* your college attendance begins. (For example, the deadline for the 2007–2008 academic year is June 30, 2008.) However, if you want to be considered for all possible types of aid, you need to fill out the form much sooner. Remember that this one form is used by many different entities to consider you for aid. To be considered for state grants, you have to complete the FAFSA by the state's deadline, and an institution's deadline for completing the FAFSA is probably much earlier than the state's. Most colleges these days have a FAFSA filing deadline that lies somewhere between February 15 and March 15 prior to the year of academic attendance.

Because of the variety of due dates and deadlines, it is a good idea to find out the earliest FAFSA deadline at all the schools you are interested in and consider that your deadline. Filing the FAFSA by the earliest deadline will help you avoid being left out of the loop. There is such a thing as filing too early, however. Applicants are not allowed to file the FAFSA before January 1 of the academic year in which they will be attending college.

CHEAP$KATE

Print and use the FAFSA on the Web Worksheet to determine your information before you complete the actual FAFSA on line. Doing the worksheet first will help you gather the right information and review for errors before you enter and submit the real FAFSA.

Tax Returns and the FAFSA

It is ideal for applicant families to have both the student's and the parents' tax returns for that fiscal year already completed and filed with the Internal Revenue Service. Sometimes, however, a family can't get this done before the FAFSA deadline. In this case, schools still recommend that you complete the FAFSA form by the deadline, using the estimated information that you do have. This information can then at least be put on file, meaning it will be less of a paperwork burden later on down the road. Online applicants and their parents can easily update their information with their actual, after-taxes figures at a later time.

Updating and Correcting the FAFSA

After your FAFSA information is processed, the result you receive is called a Student Aid Report (SAR) acknowledgement. It is important for you to review the information on your SAR and make any necessary corrections or updates as soon as possible or to notify your financial aid administrator to make these changes. Accurate information is necessary in order for you to receive the financial aid you are entitled to.

Updating Financial Information

There are a couple of ways to update your information. If you filled out the FAFSA on paper, you can mark your corrections on the SAR that you received in the mail and send the form back to the federal processor. If you completed the FAFSA online, then you can go back to the Web and correct your information. You can also contact each college and university that received a report and inform them of your updated information. They can make the corrections for you.

Sending the Information to Colleges

Applicants are allowed to have their FAFSA results sent to up to four schools at once if they file the paper FAFSA, or to six schools if they file electronically. To send your results to more than six schools, you should opt to use the online version—it is a much quicker and easier way to add schools. Just wait a couple of days, and then do a FAFSA correction, replacing the schools you originally listed with new ones. If you have filed the FAFSA on paper and you decide you want to have more schools receive your info, you will need to replace the schools on your SAR and mail the form back to the federal processor.

Another way to get your financial information to a college or university that you did not list originally is to provide the financial aid office with a hard copy of your SAR. (You can print one from the FAFSA Web site if you applied online.) The hard copy must include something called your data release number (DRN). When you provide a school with a copy of this information, you are also giving them your permission to request your FAFSA information for themselves.

No matter how you add schools to your FAFSA, the schools you add will replace schools you listed originally. In other words, the original schools will stop receiving updates when they are replaced with other schools. That's not really a problem, though. If you have provided an institution with any one version of your FAFSA in a given year, they can request the updated versions. In subsequent years, you will only need to put the one school you are attending on the FAFSA, making this part of the process a lot easier.

FACTS ABOUT FINANCIAL AID PACKAGES

A financial aid "package" is basically a list of all of the available financial aid that a particular student applicant qualifies for at a particular institution. (This determination is often based upon an applicant's FAFSA results.) Usually, the financial aid package comes in the mail, in the form of a long letter explaining the various types of financial aid options listed in the package.

The Contents of a Financial Aid Package

The items included in a financial aid package are basically a compilation of the different options that a student applicant qualifies for. A student may choose from the options offered by that particular school. The options may include some of the following types of aid:

- Federal Pell Grant
- Federal Supplemental Educational Opportunity Grant (SEOG)
- Federal Academic Competitiveness Grant (ACG)
- Academic or athletic scholarship
- Federal work-study
- State grant
- Stafford or Direct Student loan
- Perkins loan

As a result of HERA, two new federal grants became available to higher-need undergraduate students who have strong academic backgrounds. An eligible student may receive an Academic Competitiveness Grant (AC Grant) of up to $750 for the first academic year of study and up to $1,300 for the second academic year of study. To be eligible for each academic year, a student must:

- be a U.S. citizen;
- be a Federal Pell Grant recipient;
- be enrolled full-time in a degree program;
- be enrolled in the first or second academic year of his or her program of study at a two-year or four-year degree-granting institution;
- have completed a rigorous secondary school program of study (after January 1, 2006, if a first-year student, and after January 1, 2005, if a second-year student);
- not have been previously enrolled in an undergraduate program if a first-year student; and
- have at least a cumulative 3.0 grade point average on a 4.0 scale for the first academic year if a second-year student.

The other new grant is the Federal National Science and Mathematics Access to Retain Talent (SMART). A National SMART Grant will provide up to $4,000 for each of the third and fourth years of undergraduate study to full-time students who are eligible for a Federal Pell Grant and who are majoring in physical, life, or computer sciences, mathematics, technology, or engineering or in a foreign language determined critical to national security. To be eligible for each academic year, a student must:

- be a U.S. citizen;
- be a Federal Pell Grant recipient;
- be enrolled full-time in a degree program;
- be enrolled in a four-year degree-granting institution;
- major in physical, life or computer science, engineering, mathematics, technology, or a critical foreign language; and
- have at least a cumulative 3.0 grade point average on a 4.0 scale

CHEAP$KATE

Thinking about registering as an independent? You must be at least one of the following to be considered an independent student: twenty-four years old or older; enrolled in a master's or doctorate program; the parent of children who receive more than half their support from you; responsible for dependents other than your children or spouse who receive more than half their support from you; the child of parents who are both deceased (or a ward of the court/state at the age of eighteen); or a veteran of, or currently serving on active duty in, the U.S. Armed Forces.

Of course, the student is in no way required to accept any or all of these options. These types of aid are discussed in detail throughout this book, so don't worry if these terms mean nothing to you at this point.

There is no rule, regulation, or law (written or otherwise) saying that a student is forbidden to refuse to accept the loans offered to him or her in a financial aid package. Chances are, though, that if you're reading this book, you're ready to take all the help you can get. Just keep in mind that you do have the right to reject any of the items listed in a financial aid package. Whether you make use of that right is completely up to you.

SAVVY STUDENTS SAVE

The cost of a postage stamp may save you some money. Write a letter to request special consideration if you have extraordinary financial circumstances, such as a reduction in income or some unusual expense. A Financial Aid Administrator may decide to use professional judgment to override some of your FAFSA data elements based on your situation.

How Many Packages Can You Get?

In the same way that every institution has its own financial aid office, different schools also have their own respective policies for awarding financial aid packages. This means that if you were to apply for a financial aid package at six different institutions of higher learning, you would probably receive six very different financial aid packages. Most schools require that you apply for admission, and be accepted, before they will determine your financial aid package, so remember to do that too!

Financial Aid Packages—A Diverse World

The expected family contribution (EFC) that is calculated for an applicant for the upcoming academic year is a fixed amount. This means that an applicant cannot change it, regardless of what college he or she eventually ends up attending. However, as you learned earlier, the factor that does vary is the actual cost of attendance at the various institutions you are considering. As a result of those costs, the demonstrated financial need for the student varies from one institution to another.

CHEAP$KATE

The total amount of a student applicant's demonstrated financial need is calculated by subtracting the expected family contribution (EFC) from the institution's total cost of attendance (COA). In other words, financial need equals COA minus EFC.

Packages Can Vary from School to School

Each college's respective financial aid office will award as much money to a student applicant as the student is qualified to receive. This qualification is based upon the individual student's demonstrated financial need *at that school*. Remember, each school has a different cost of attendance, so a student may get extremely different total financial aid amounts for different schools.

Here's an example. Suppose your EFC is calculated to be $2,000. Let's say you apply to School A, where the cost of attendance is $12,000, and to School B, where the cost of attendance is $32,000. Here is what the two financial aid packages might look like:

Some schools may require additional forms before they award financial aid, such as the College Scholarship Service (CSS) profile. There is a nominal registration fee to complete the CSS profile and a per-school fee to send the results to institutions. So make sure a school requires the form before you pay for it and have the information sent to them. See *http://profileonline.collegeboard.com* for more information.

School A:
Pell Grant: $2,360
Federal work-study: $1,800
State grant: $500
Federal Stafford loan: $3,500
Federal Perkins loan: $1,000
Total aid: $9,160
Difference that family must pay or borrow for
    School A: $2,840

School B:
Academic scholarship: $10,000
College need-based grant: $5,000
Pell Grant: $2,360
Supplemental Educational Opportunity Grant
    (SEOG): $1,500
Federal work-study: $2,300
State grant: $3,500
Federal Stafford loan: $3,500
Federal Perkins loan: $2,000
Total aid: $30,160
Difference that family must pay or borrow at
    School B: $1,840

Even though School B looks more expensive at the outset, with financial aid packages like these, it will actually be more affordable for the student to attend School B.

Will Qualifications Change If You Change Schools?

As a student applicant, you can qualify for certain forms of financial aid that will remain in place regardless of what school(s) you attend between freshman year and graduation. This is true as long as your financial need does not change from one year to the next. For example, your Pell Grant is not likely to change as long as you were a full-time student at some college and as long as your EFC is the same each year you complete the FAFSA.

However, there are other monetary amounts that might end up differing as you go from one school's financial aid options to another's because schools have more discretion in awarding those funds. This includes options such as the SEOG (Supplemental Educational Opportunity Grant), state grants, scholarship awards, work-study programs, and tuition loans. Check with each school's financial aid office to see whether your package will be affected in future years if your EFC stays the same.

SAVVY STUDENTS SAVE

It is a good idea to shop around when you make any major purchase. Your education is no different. Shop around to find the best fit and the best value for your money. In the end, you may end up paying a little more, but you might be getting a lot more for your money.

HOW CAN YOU QUALIFY?

Some of the items in the financial aid package are actually awards from what are referred to as "campus-based" programs, such as the Supplemental Educational Opportunity Grants, federal work-study programs, and Perkins loans. These are federal financial aid programs that are administered directly by the financial aid offices at each participating school. In other words, the institution gets an allotment from the U.S. federal government. It is up to the school to distribute the funds, and each institution can determine how it allocates the money it receives to its students (according to a set of a few short, very basic guidelines). That is why a student might end up receiving different amounts of these funds, depending upon what school the package comes from. When a school uses up its allocation for that academic year, the money is gone, and no more awards can be given out from the program that year.

SAVVY STUDENTS SAVE

If a student qualifies for additional grants or scholarships after a financial aid package has been determined, it may affect some of the existing aid. In some cases, existing aid must be adjusted to stay within amounts allowed by federal regulations. It is a good idea to ask each institution you are considering what their policy is regarding outside scholarships.

Also, when it comes to financial aid funds, institutions are not very tightly regulated concerning how they spend their own money. As a result, different schools have very different amounts of money set aside in their budgets for student financial aid. Different institutions will also have their own policies for just how they think that money should be spent. In other words, a student might be awarded a large institutional scholarship in one school's financial aid package but absolutely no scholarship award whatsoever at another.

It is always a smart idea to hold off on evaluating the bottom-line costs at different schools until after you have received the financial aid packages from all of your schools. Why? With all the facts in front of you, you can make a truly informed decision—one based upon the actual cost (the cost you pay) to attend the different schools you are considering.

Grad Students Use the FAFSA Too

The financial aid process for the adult graduate student is pretty much the same as for an undergraduate student. The main difference is that a student in graduate or professional school is automatically considered to be independent, so the parents' income no longer counts toward financial aid calculations.

Graduate-level students who wish to receive federal financial aid or grants must file a FAFSA stating that they are pursuing a master's or doctorate degree (or have entered some other graduate study program). To continue receiving aid, students must indicate the same continuing education on the FAFSA renewal forms. Graduate level students are also eligible to receive Stafford loans, Perkins loans, and federal work-study. This means filling out a FAFSA is definitely in your best interests. After all, every little bit helps!

Chapter 6

CONSIDER THIS: QUALIFIED TUITION PLANS AND FEDERAL INCOME TAX BENEFITS

Qualified tuition plans? Section 529 plans? Sound confusing? It's not as bad as you might think. In fact, you should get to know this type of plan (they mean the same thing, by the way) as it is a very good tool for families to use in meeting the financial part of their college goals for their children. While Section 529 plans help families prepare for the cost of college, tax benefits help families save tax dollars. Remember, "free money" can take many forms. A dollar <u>not spent</u> is a dollar <u>saved!</u>

WHAT ARE 529 PLANS?

Section 529 plans are savings plans operated by state governments (or eligible educational institutions). They are usually managed by established investment companies. They can be set up to prepay tuition or contribute to a current or future student's education. One of the best factors of 529 plans is that as you save up college money, you also get some nice tax exemptions.

These plans are set up under the Internal Revenue Code Section 529 (hence the name) as part of the 2001 Tax Relief Act. (Look, the word "relief" is in there!) There are two main types of Section 529 plans—prepaid tuition plans and college savings plans. When these plans were first implemented, many states offered the prepaid tuition option to their residents. Unfortunately, the average rate of increase for college tuition was greater than the growth rate of funds in these plans. Because the prepaid plan couldn't keep up with these tuition increases, states began to move away from this option.

These days, most Section 529 plans are college savings plans, which are very similar to just about any other type of investment vehicle. Investment vehicle? You might ask . . . well, think of it this way—you put your money into the plan and (hopefully) watch it start to grow. In this case, you really are *investing* in your future!

Advantages of College Savings Plans

The HERA's changes to college savings plans now means that all qualified educational benefit plans, including Section 529 plans, other prepaid tuition plans offered by a state, and Coverdell education savings accounts can be reported as an asset of either the student or the parent (the amount reported for a state prepaid tuition plan is the refund value of the plan). Let's look at some different types of assets:

Parent Asset: If the student is dependent and the parents have funds in one of these types of accounts, the current value in the account should be reported as a parent asset on the FAFSA.

Not Reported: If the student is dependent and the student has funds in one of these types of accounts, the current value in the account should not be reported on the FAFSA.

Student Asset: If the student is independent and the student or the student's spouse has funds in one of these types of accounts, the current value in the account should be reported as a student/spouse asset on the FAFSA.

CHEAP$KATE

Lucky for you and students all over the country, each of the fifty states is currently participating in Section 529 plans for college tuition assistance. This means that no matter where you live or attend school, they are there to be found. Take a look.

A college savings plan may provide you with more options than a prepaid tuition plan because it gives you greater flexibility in your choice of colleges. This is a significant advantage when you consider that a savings plan can start ten to fifteen years (sometimes more) before you even start looking at colleges and considering your options!

Common Traits of Section 529 Plans

No matter which type of Section 529 plan you end up with, there are some important features you should know about. It is always good to know as much as you can when it comes to investment planning. If you know what you're getting into, you're less likely to get blindsided later on. Here are some of the basic facts to remember about Section 529 plans:

- Earnings from Section 529 plans are exempt from federal taxes, as are withdrawals used for paying college costs.
- Some states also waive state tax for residents, while others allow deductions on contributions.
- Section 529 plans have generous maximum contribution limits, as much as $250,000 per beneficiary.
- Most states hire investment companies to manage these plans, for maximum investment efficiency and return.
- Funds withdrawn for purposes other than education are subject to a 10 percent penalty and to federal income taxes. (States assess their own penalties.)

Don't forget, Section 529 plans change depending upon your state of residence. Depending on where you live, some of the above factors may not apply. However, being aware of the most common factors will at least empower you to ask your Section 529 plan provider about which of these traits will apply to your specific situation. You can stay in the game if you ask the right questions!

Get the Grandparents Involved!

Section 529 plans are a really good idea for parents who are saving for a child's college education. But it doesn't just have to be parents! They also allow for contributions by grandparents and anyone else who wants to help. Saving money now could mean borrowing a lot less money later (which translates into a lot less to be paid back—with interest). With Section 529 plans, grandparents enjoy a tax benefit while providing their grandchildren money to help pay for education.

Section 529 plans have grown into one of the most popular methods for families to start saving for their children's college education. Though these plans may be different from one state to another, they are all exempt from federal income tax, and that could translate into one heck of a contribution to a student's college fund.

QUALIFIED EDUCATION EXPENSES

The money in a Section 529 plan should be dedicated to paying "qualified education expenses." What qualifies as "qualified?" you might ask. Expenses include tuition, fees, books, course supplies, room and board, and required course equipment. All of these expenses must be charged by an institution the U.S. Department of Education considers to be eligible for participation. The student must also be enrolled at least half time at this accredited institution. Don't forget these key things—'cause that saved money is useless if you don't know the rules!

Qualified educational expenses are reduced by any tax-free financial aid the student receives, such as tax-free scholarships, veterans' benefits, Pell grants, employer-provided educational assistance, and other nontaxable forms of educational assistance. The taxable part is based on the difference between the total of the distributions and the adjusted qualified educational expenses. See IRS Publication 970, *Tax Benefits for Higher Education* (available on the Web at *www.irs.gov*), for an explanation of how to determine the amount of qualified educational expenses you have.

IMPROPER USE

Since they were introduced in 1996, thousands of investors have taken advantage of Section 529 plans and the way that contributions to the accounts remain tax-free as they grow. Some people take further advantage of the fact that withdrawals stay free from federal tax as long as the funds are used for education expenses.

When Section 529 plans were first thought up, the intention was to help those who had already stashed away some money for their children's educations. Unfortunately, changes introduced in 2001 have begun to allow many investors to start bending the original rules. Unfortunately, this has caused a problem for Section 529 plans. They have begun to attract investors who have no intention of using the account to put their children through college.

Not long after the new tax laws of 2001 were put into action, many financial advisers began working out ways for clients to take creative tax advantages from them. As it turned out, Section 529 plans worked really well if used as estate-planning tools because they let the individual investor move quite a bit more money in and out of an estate. Why? After the 2001 tax exemptions, investors could take large amounts of money out of an estate, a lot more than would be normally allowed without incurring some amount of penalty in terms of federal gift taxes.

Most Section 529 plans are controlled by professional, experienced fund managers. That takes a little bit of the risk out of your investment, especially if you are not investment-savvy or if you do not have enough time to regularly oversee your own investment account. As with all investments, there is no guarantee that you will not end up taking a loss, but at least with a certified fund manager, you'll be less likely to blame yourself if there is one.

Isn't That Illegal?

You would think that taking advantage of educational savings plans with no intention of using the money for education would be illegal, but the sad truth is that it is not. The practices just described, though somewhat unethical, are not considered illegal by the federal government or the Internal Revenue Service. Can you believe it? The "creative" use of Section 529 plans has yet to cause enough of a strain in governmental tax losses to be considered as illegal tax evasion by the IRS. Does that mean it never will? Absolutely not!

Don't Try It!

If you are going to take advantage of a Section 529 plan, be sure you do so ethically—to pay your student's college tuition! These so-called "creative" investors are in the clear for now because there are currently no laws set down to deter them. They will probably end up getting nailed by the IRS soon enough, especially once old Uncle Sam realizes just how much money he's losing in tax dollars and decides to assemble a federal task force to crack down on Section 529 abusers. Don't get in this mess!

SAVVY STUDENTS SAVE

In addition to tax incentives, Section 529 plans include many other benefits. They can be used for graduate or undergraduate education, the contributions are transferable, contribution limits are high, and there is no age limit on their use.

SECTION 529 TAX BENEFITS

In addition to the obvious benefit of having money available for your student's college education, Section 529 plans offer tax relief as well. Since it took effect in January of 2002, the Tax Relief Act of 2001 has made Section 529 plans appealing to many people, whether they have a college-bound child or not. In fact, not only are there tax benefits on the account's interest (earnings), there also may be benefits on the money you put into the account (contributions), and money you take out (distributions). Let's take a closer look into these benefits.

Account Earnings

As of 2006, all of the earnings from a Section 529 plan account are exempt from federal tax, as long as they are eventually withdrawn for the exclusive use of paying for qualified education expenses. This means that unlike the taxes an investor is normally required to pay on earnings from most types of investments, no taxes are paid on the interest earned by money invested in a Section 529 plan. This holds true unless you withdraw the money for uses other than your student's higher education. Section 529 plan earnings are currently tax-deferred in nearly all states as well, meaning you don't pay taxes on the money as long as it is in a 529. It can't hurt to find out more, right? Why not ask your Section 529 provider if your state gives these tax deferrals?

The Pension Protection Act of 2006

Now the income tax exclusion for qualified withdrawals from Section 529 plans is permanent thanks to the Pension Protection Act of 2006. With college costs continuing to rise, the assurance of tax incentives through these types of plans makes them an even better investment. This Act also allows rollovers from one account to another every 12 months (including same-beneficiary rollovers), eliminates the mandated state penalties on non-qualified distributions, expands eligible family members to include first cousins for rollovers and beneficiary changes, and maintains the state income tax exclusion for those states that follow the federal tax treatment of Section 529 plans.

CHEAP$KATE

The assets in a Section 529 plan belong to the owner of the plan, not to the student beneficiary. This works in the student's favor! If a parent is the owner of the plan, then the assets must be reported as a parent asset on the FAFSA (and is assessed at a lower percentage than a student asset in the formula). If someone other than the parent or student is the owner of the plan, it should not be reported as an asset of either the parent or student on the FAFSA.

Contributions and Distributions

As mentioned earlier, a tax break on your Section 529 earnings is only one of the tax advantages that comes with using these plans. Section 529 contributions are not pre-taxed, meaning you do not pay state or federal tax on money deposited into an account. Some states also allow you to deduct a set portion of your contributions from state tax.

SAVVY STUDENTS SAVE

The U.S. Securities and Exchange Commission has an easy-to-understand introduction to 529 plans that is available online at *www.sec.gov/investor/pubs/intro529.htm*.

Generally, distributions (withdrawals) are also tax-free, as long as you don't take out more than the amount equal to the beneficiary's adjusted qualified tuition expenses. Anything above and beyond that amount will be taxed. Again, ask your 529 provider about what your state's particular policies are before you start counting on receiving these exemptions—but, if you choose to use this plan, you should get some great breaks!

OTHER EDUCATION TAX BENEFITS

In addition to the tax benefits of a Section 529 plan, the other educational tax benefits currently authorized by the IRS are the Hope Scholarship Tax Credit, the Lifetime Learning Tax Credit, and the Tuition and Fees Tax Deduction. For each of these plans, tax credits are subtracted directly from a taxpayer's federal tax obligation. A tax deduction is subtracted from taxable income. Let's take a closer look at each of these avenues for saving.

The Hope Scholarship Tax Credit

If you file a federal tax return and owe taxes, then this credit may be possible. In 2007, for the 2006 tax-filing year, a family can claim a tax credit for up to two years in the amount of $1,650 for each dependent. That's figured at 100 percent of the first $1,100 and 50 percent of the second $1,100 you paid out in qualified educational expenses. In order to qualify for this tax credit, there are some additional stipulations you must meet. The eligible student must be the taxpayer, the taxpayer's spouse, or the taxpayer's dependent as claimed on the taxpayer's tax return. There is an adjusted gross income limit of $55,000 if filing single and $110,000 if married and filing a joint tax return. (These amounts are a few thousand dollars higher than they were in the previous tax year.) Taxpayers with incomes over these levels do not qualify for the Hope Scholarship Tax Credit.

Stay Ahead of the Game

If you are close to the income level restrictions for a tax benefit, be sure to pay attention to changes in tax regulations each year. Income level limitations may change, which means you might not qualify in one year, but may qualify the next year.

To be considered an eligible student for a Hope Scholarship Tax Credit, you must be enrolled in the first two years of a degree or certificate program. You also must be enrolled at least half-time for at least one academic period of enrollment (semester or term). The institution you are attending must be a college, university, vocational school, or other postsecondary educational institution eligible to participate in a U.S. federal student aid program. Fortunately, this includes virtually all post-secondary institutions in the United States.

SAVVY STUDENTS SAVE

Pay attention to *when* you make your qualified education payments. The Hope Scholarship Tax Credit includes expenses paid in a *calendar* year. The timing of your tuition bill should be considered when you get your semester bill. For example, it might work to your advantage to pay for second semester charges prior to December 31 in a calendar year so you can count those qualified education expenses in that year (or wait until after January 1 to count them in the next calendar year).

To claim this tax credit, you need to complete an IRS form 8863. This form collects the amount of tuition and fees you paid, as well as the amount of scholarships, grants, etc. that were used to pay the qualified expenses.

Colleges and universities are required to send you a form 1098-T statement by January 31 each year to help you determine these figures.

Try Lifetime Learning!

The name of this program is Lifetime Learning, right? What do you think that means? It can help you no matter what your age or schooling level? You're right! Unlike the Hope Scholarship Tax Credit, which is available only for a student's first two years of college, the Lifetime Learning Tax Credit is available for all years of college and also for courses that improve job skills. In this program a tax payment may claim a tax credit of up to $2,000 per year per taxpayer family. The student must be the taxpayer, the taxpayer's spouse, or the taxpayer's dependent student as shown on the taxpayer's tax return.

The amount of Lifetime Learning Tax Credit allowed is 20 percent of the first $10,000 of qualified educational expenses paid for all eligible students, which equals a maximum of $2,000. The same income restrictions apply for the Lifetime Learning Tax Credit as for the Hope Scholarship Tax Credit—$55,000 for a single taxpayer and $110,000 for married taxpayers filing a joint return.

Also like the Hope Scholarship Tax Credit, an IRS form 8863 is required using qualified education expenses reported on the form 1098-T that the institution must provide to you by January 31 each year.

What About Double Dipping?

The exclusion from gross income provided by distributions from Section 529 plans, coupled with the Hope Scholarship Tax Credit and the Lifetime Learning Tax Credit, should mean the same expenses can be counted as many as three times to get triple the amount of "free money" off your tax obligation. Unfortunately, the federal government doesn't want us double counting any dollars spent when calculating tax benefits. A family may claim more than one of these tax benefits, as long as the same student is not used as the basis for each credit or Section 529 exclusion and the family is within the Lifetime Learning maximum per family.

Stay Ahead of the Game

Print the following free IRS publications from the Internet and refer to them when completing your federal income tax return: Publication 970 Tax Benefits for Higher Education, Form 8863 and Instructions, Education Credits (Hope and Lifetime Learning Credits), Tax Topic 605, Education Credits, and Frequently Asked Questions and Answers from the IRS, Education Tax Credits.

TUITION AND FEES TAX DEDUCTION— ONE MORE WAY TO SAVE TAX DOLLARS

Which one is unlike the others? This one! The Tuition and Fees Tax Deduction does not reduce your tax obligation like the Hope Scholarship and Lifetime Learning Tax Credits do. Instead, this tax benefit reduces your taxable income by as much as $4,000 in 2006. You are allowed to utilize this deduction even if you do not itemize deductions. Up to $4,000 can be claimed by taxpayers with adjusted gross incomes of $65,000 or less if filing single, or adjusted gross incomes of $130,000 or less for married couples filing joint returns. If adjusted income is greater than $65,000 and $80,000 for single filers, or between $130,000 and $160,000 for joint filers, then the tax deduction is limited to $2,000 maximum.

Obviously, with higher income level limitations than the tax credit programs, this tax deduction enables families that do not qualify for the tax credits to still claim some tax benefit from their education-related spending. If your income levels and educational expenses fall within any of these tax credit or deduction program guidelines, you have an easy, guaranteed way to save some cash!

Chapter 7

LEANING ON LOANS

Scholarships, grants, tax credits—they're all great, but these things can't make it possible for everyone to go to school. For most students, paying for college involves taking out some kind of loan. This should not necessarily be considered a bad thing. People borrow money for many big events in their lives—to buy a car, a home, or even start a business. Paying for a college education is one more reason people look to take out loans. The important thing is that students and parents become informed as borrowers so they know how to choose the best loan with the lowest interest rate and best payback benefits for their individual situations. Let's take a closer look at specific loans and how they can help you. And as the saying goes, "if the shoe fits . . . " why not start working on getting those funds fast?

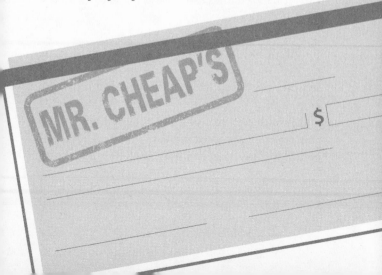

THE STAFFORD LOAN—
PAID BACK AFTER SCHOOL

One of the most well-know loans is The Stafford loan. It is a federal loan that is available to both undergraduate and graduate college students. This loan is granted completely in the student's name. No co-signer is required or allowed (this is important!). In order to take out a Stafford loan, the student must sign a promissory note—a binding legal document that specifies the obligations that come with the loan.

The Stafford loan can come in one of two forms: a direct Stafford loan or a Federal Family Education Loan (or FFEL) Stafford loan. Basically, these are the same loan, at least from the student's perspective. The difference is that direct Stafford loans are borrowed directly from the college or university, while FFEL Stafford loans are borrowed through a private lending institution (such as a bank or credit union) that participates in the FFEL Stafford loan program. Students must repay the direct Stafford loans to the federal government, but FFEL Stafford loans are repaid to the private lender's designated agency or financial institution.

Stafford Loan Payments

Payment on a Stafford loan is deferred (meaning no payments are due) until after the student graduates or ceases to be at least a half-time student. ("Half time" is a course load of six credit hours, or roughly two courses per semester.) Stafford loans disbursed after July 1, 2006 have a fixed interest rate of 6.8 percent, which is currently a very good interest rate. Based on repayment plan choice and amount owed, if you take out one of these loans, you could have up to ten to twenty-five years to repay! That's pretty nice.

Subsidized Versus Unsubsidized

Don't forget that your qualification for the subsidized or the unsubsidized version will be determined through your FAFSA information—so fill it out! It will also depend upon the other types and amounts of financial aid you already qualify for.

Note: A student's Stafford loan may be subsidized or unsubsidized. The subsidized Stafford loan is a little better because the government pays off (or "subsidizes") the interest on your loan while you are attending college. Subsidized loans are awarded based upon financial need, and students can get need-based financial aid only up to their official demonstrated need (the school's cost of attendance minus your expected family contribution).

If you do not qualify for the subsidized Stafford loan, you can still get an unsubsidized loan, which does not require demonstration of financial need. Interest on unsubsidized Stafford loans starts to accrue from the moment you take out the loan. With the unsubsidized Stafford loan, you have the option of allowing the interest to capitalize (in which case it is added to the principal that you will repay later) or paying off the interest amount in installments on a quarterly basis. Think about what is best for you and your family—no matter what your situation, you have options!

Don't miss it! For standard, fall enrollment freshmen matriculation, a typical loan-processing timeline for federal Stafford and PLUS loans for fall enrollment would begin when the borrower completes his or her application in May or June. The financial aid office would then certify the loan sometime during the month of August, in time for you to avoid late fees on your bill.

How Much Can You Borrow?

It would be great if there weren't borrowing limits to Stafford Loans. but unfortunately the amount of a Stafford loan is restricted, based upon the student's year in college. Included in the HERA changes, Congress set the annual amount of federal Stafford money that an undergraduate dependent student can borrow at the following limits: $3,500 for freshmen; $4,500 for sophomores; and $5,500 for juniors and seniors. Graduate and professional degree students can borrow as much as $20,500 per year, regardless of their years in a program, as long as no more than $8,500 of the annual amount is subsidized. This is an increase for freshman and sophomores from previous years, so consider yourself lucky!

Beyond these basic loan limits, an undergraduate student can borrow as much as an additional $4,000 each year as a freshmen or sophomore student, and an additional $5,000 more each year as a junior or senior. These additional funds are available if the student's parent has been denied a PLUS loan. Dependent undergraduates can borrow up to a total of $23,000 and independent undergraduate can borrow up to $46,000 (but no more than $23,000 can be subsidized). A graduate or professional degree student's maximum total debt limit is $138,500, with no more than $65,500 of this amount in subsidized loans.

Schools are required to divide the award of a Stafford loan into at least two installments, which are typically paid in each semester of the academic year. Funds are distributed to the student, less a small loan-origination fee that is usually deducted each semester. Your direct educational expenses must be paid off before anything else (tuition and fees plus room and board). Once these have been paid, if any money is left, it may be used toward some of your other, non-comprehensive charges and expenses, such as rent, utilities, books, transportation, and personal expenses.

SAVVY STUDENTS SAVE

If you are a student returning to college, you must not be in default status on any past federal Perkins loans, direct loans, or FFEL Stafford loans. This is an easy way to get into trouble . . . if you are in default status and have not already made satisfactory arrangements for repayment of your past debt, you will not be eligible for any federal financial aid until your default status is resolved. Don't let this happen to you!

THE PERKINS LOAN—
ARE YOU ELIGIBLE?

The Perkins loan is another federal program that works for both undergraduate and graduate students. Similar to the Stafford loans, no co-signer is required. Unlike a Stafford loan, the Perkins program is campus-based (as are the Supplemental Educational Opportunity Grant or, better known as, the federal work-study programs). The government allocates funds to the institution, and it is the responsibility of the institution to set its own policy regarding who receives a loan. In order to be eligible to receive a Perkins loan, the student must have a certain amount of demonstrated financial need. The Perkins loan places the college or university in the role of lender, which means you must pay the money back to your school when the time comes to repay the loan.

Perkins loans are subsidized, which means no interest accrues as long as you are enrolled in enough courses to qualify as at least a half-time student. When the student finally repays the loan, interest begins to accrue at a set rate of 5 percent. Not bad, right? Let's take a closer look. Here are some basics things you should know about the Perkins loans:

- There are no loan origination fees for a Perkins loan.
- Loan limits are set at $4,000 for each year of undergraduate study (with no more than $20,000 borrowed total), and $6,000 for each year of graduate study (up to $40,000 total).

However, keep in mind that it is very uncommon for educational institutions to have enough money in their budgets to award the federal maximum to their students. The amount you receive depends on your EFC, official need, and the school's level of funding. So this might be something to think about (and ask about) when you are looking at different colleges and making that all important apples-to-apples list.

PAYING LOANS BACK

The federal government is more than happy to "give out" money—as long as the person they give it to has to pay the money back! Here is a little tip on the way the federal government handles money matters—when it comes to distributing your loan, they will take their sweet time! The funny thing is, when it comes time for you to pay them, they want their money, and they want it right away. Does this mean federal loans are the wrong way to go? Absolutely not. You just need to know what you are getting into.

CHEAP$KATE

The Student Guide is a free annual publication. Printed by the U.S. Department of Education, it contains valuable information about all kinds of federal financial aid programs, including federal loans, their interest rates, and what your repayment obligations will be. The current publication can be viewed online, and it is also available in print at almost any college or university.

Forgiveness of Federal Loans

In certain cases, if a student meets the right requirements, part of an outstanding Stafford or Perkins loan can be canceled, which would be absolutely terrific for a recent graduate just starting out in the "real world." For example, as much as $5,000 of a Stafford loan can be forgiven (and never have to be paid) if the student is employed as a full-time teacher for at least five consecutive years at certain elementary or secondary schools whose students come primarily from low-income families. A portion of your Perkins loan might also be forgiven if you serve as a

Vista or Peace Corps volunteer or if you are a member of the U.S. Armed Forces and serving in a hostile area.

Any Chance the Whole Loan Be Forgiven?

Yes! As much as 100 percent of a Perkins loan can be forgiven if you are a teacher and there is a teacher shortage in your specialty. This may also be an option if you are a full-time nurse or medical technician, a full-time law enforcement officer, or another type of corrections officer.

Could Someone Show Me Some Grace, Please?

Federal Stafford and Perkins loans have a grace period associated with them. A grace period is when you are not required to make any payments. It begins when you graduate or withdraw or drop below half-time enrollment status. Be careful about any decision to take a break from your studies because you are only allowed one grace period. The Stafford Loan grace period is 6 months from the time you are no longer a full-time student until your first payment is due. The Perkins loan grace period is 9 months from the time you are no longer a full-time student until your first payment is due.

One thing you definitely don't want to do is go into default on any student loan. Even one late payment can mark your account "delinquent." If you are 90 or more days delinquent, the national credit bureaus are informed and it's a big black mark on your credit history. More than 270 days late in making a student loan payment and your loan will be in "default." A loan default stays on your credit record for seven long years. This means you may not be able to get other loans, such as a car loan, mortgage, or additional student loans.

PARENT'S HELP IN THEIR OWN WAY—PLUS LOANS

PLUS loans are for parents of dependent undergraduate students who are enrolled in college as at least half-time students. Unlike the federal loans we have already discussed, this particular loan is taken in the parent's name instead of the student's. Parent borrowers may be denied approval for PLUS loans, however, if one or both parents have an adverse credit history. But if parents have good credit, this kind of loan can be perfect for some families! Why so great, you ask? Take a closer look below.

Just like the different kinds of Stafford loans, there are FFEL PLUS loans as well as direct PLUS loans. With a direct PLUS program, parents borrow from the federal government through the college or university or through a private lending institution. The college or university participates in either one or the other type of PLUS program. The financial aid office can supply instructions to parents on how to apply.

CHEAP$KATE

The Parent Loan for Undergraduate Students (PLUS) is easier to qualify for than some other types of loans because the credit check is based upon federal standards. There are no debt-to-income ratios or credit scoring involved in qualifying for a PLUS loan.

PLUS Interest Rates

The interest rate for a PLUS loan is fixed at 8.5 percent, and it's important to know that it's quite a bit higher than the rate of a Stafford or Perkins loan. However, the

PLUS loan may have higher borrowing limits than the Stafford or Perkins loan. Let's take a look at the pros and cons.

PLUS Advantages and Disadvantages

One of the biggest advantages of having a PLUS loan is that the parent is able to borrow an amount equal to the cost of education (after any other financial aid the student receives is subtracted from this amount). In other words, the parent can borrow up to the expected family contribution on the FAFSA as well as anything that is not covered by certain other types of financial aid.

But you must keep in mind that one big disadvantage of a PLUS loan is that parents have to start paying the loan back a lot earlier. Payment installments must begin within sixty days—yes, days—after the loan has been fully disbursed for one academic year.

SAVVY STUDENTS SAVE

Don't forget to get your tax deduction for interest paid on student loans, including PLUS loans. Currently the maximum deduction is a whopping $2,500 a year!

If the parent of a student is denied for a PLUS loan, then the student's educational institution is authorized to automatically award the student as much as $4,000 to $5,000 (for undergraduate freshmen and sophomores or juniors and seniors, respectively) in the form of additional, unsubsidized Stafford loan funds. So if the PLUS loans aren't for your family, don't think you're just left out in the cold!

The law now allows graduate and professional degree students to borrow from the PLUS loan program also. As with parent borrowers, eligible graduate and professional degree students may borrow up to their cost of attendance, minus other financial aid received. Unlike parent borrowers, graduate and professional degree borrowers must complete a FAFSA and have their eligibility under the Stafford loan program determined before borrowing a PLUS loan. But if your forms show that you truly are eligible, you're good to go! It's sure worth a shot.

THERE ARE MANY LOAN OPTIONS!

Alternative loan programs are student educational loans that are funded through either a bank or other lending institution. Most of the time, these loans are made in the student's name. Unlike loans such as the Stafford or Perkins, however, a creditworthy co-signer is usually required for the loan to be approved. Different lending institutions have different loan minimums, maximums, and borrower benefits. With a creditworthy co-signer, most of these loans let the student borrow the total cost of attendance minus any other financial aid that they receive.

There are too many alternative loan options for most students and parents to sort through on their own, so most colleges and universities were providing a valuable service to families by publishing a list of favorable loan options; however, it was discovered that a few colleges were using questionable (and even unethical) practices regarding student loan policies. For example, some institutions required students to use a particular loan or lender, even if that was not the student's choice or did not provide the most favorable borrower benefits. Investigations in 2006 led to new legislation that regulates how much "guidance" an institution can give to borrowers of private loans.

On February 7, 2007, H.R. 890, the Student Loan Sunshine Act, was introduced to establish requirements for lenders and institutions of higher education in order to protect students and other borrowers receiving educational loans. The Act passed by the U.S. House of Representatives on May 9, 2007. If voted on by the Senate and signed by the President, the law would require each lender entering into an educational loan arrangement with a postsecondary school to:

1. Report annually to the Secretary of Education specified information concerning such an arrangement;
2. Inform borrowers of their loan options under title IV before extending private educational loans for attendance at such school; and
3. Be barred by such school from marketing such loans in a manner implying the school's endorsement.

The law would also require schools that provide prospective borrowers with private educational loan information to:

1. Include information on their title IV assistance eligibility; and
2. Compare and distinguish private loans from title IV loans.

What all of this means to students and parents is that you can still seek guidance from the college or university regarding your alternative loan options, but make sure you understand how the school selected those loan options for recommendation. Don't blindly use a lender just because a college financial aid administrator recommends that lender! Get more involved and your choices will pay off more in the end. Become educated in what to look for when choosing loans and then make the best decision for the person who will end up paying back that loan—you!

Ideally, institutions and borrowers should evaluate alternative loans based on interest rates, fees charged, interest rate reduction options, co-signer release options, savings potential, and other borrower benefits (such as borrower age requirement, loans for past-due balances, academic progress requirements). If you are confident that your college or university has done the research and their recommendations are in your best interest, then it has saved you much time and trouble. It's important that you do at least enough research to know this for sure.

SAVVY STUDENTS SAVE

With some alternative loans, it is possible to release the co-signer from the loan obligation once the student has made a certain number of regularly scheduled payments, in full and on time. If you are responsible about making your payments, you can take some of the debt load off your parents—and maybe free them to take out a loan of their own.

Advantages and Disadvantages

Okay, we all know that an additional loan is never desirable. In fact, you should avoid it at all costs. However, sometimes it is necessary, and if you keep your head on straight and borrow only what you need, it can fill the gap in your costs and payments. An advantage to having an alternative student loan is that your repayment is often deferred until after you have graduated from college. This is because as a student, you are listed as the primary borrower, and it is therefore your responsibility to repay your loan. The bank understands that this probably isn't possible while you are still in school, when you are unlikely to have *any* cash in your pockets at all.

On the other hand, one of the disadvantages to having an alternative student loan is that the parent (or whoever your co-signer might have been) is held responsible for paying the loan back if for some reason you do not. This can be a huge problem if neither you, nor your co-signer, can make the payments once you graduate and the loan needs to be repaid. Not making the loan payments can ruin the credit of the borrower and the co-signer. What a way to lose face with friends and relatives!

CHEAP$KATE

It's a good idea to ask an institution for its policy for providing loan information. That will help you know to what degree the school researches the available loans before making any recommendations to students and parents. The more you know, the better off you are. Take the time to research—it'll pay off!

Even More Loan Options

Remember that everyone is different, and there is no "umbrella loan" that just works for anybody and everybody. You don't have to settle for what is initially made available to you. Do plenty of checking, and you will be able to sign your loan promissory note with the confidence that comes from knowing your options—and knowing that the loan you finally chose was the very best loan for you. Like it or not, you need to do some of the same type of comparison shopping you did when choosing a school. Create a comparison chart, add information as you gather it, and make an alternative loan decision that fits within your financial boundaries (remember those?).

Group 'em Together Through Student Loan Consolidation

After you graduate, you can consider loan consolidation. Basically, this means taking out one big new loan that combines (or consolidates) all your different federal student loans, with the benefit of giving you one loan payment to worry about. By taking out the consolidation loan, you get to pay off existing loans and then concentrate on repaying the consolidation loan. There are a few lenders that will consolidate private, non-federal loans, but be careful, they may have exorbitant interest rates.

SAVVY STUDENTS SAVE

Before you consolidate your loans, talk to the holders of your loans to make sure you aren't giving up benefits that make your unconsolidated loan more beneficial to you than a consolidation one (such as interest rate discounts, principal rebates, or Perkins loan discharge or cancellation benefits).

Student loan consolidation can significantly lower your monthly payments by extending the duration of your loan's terms, often without incurring any prepayment penalties. Consolidation makes the most sense if you can get a better interest rate than what you're currently paying on your smaller loans. Even with a lower monthly payment, consolidation won't make much sense in the long run if it means paying a lot more in interest than you would have otherwise. You may also extend your repayment term on federal loans and receive a fixed interest rate on any variable rate loans taken prior to July 1, 2006. Talk to a loan counselor or someone in the financial aid office, it can't hurt.

The consolidation process is often very easy, and in some cases it can even be done for free. In this context, "free" means that you won't be charged any additional loan-related fees. This does not mean that your new creditor will pay off your loans for free (so don't ask them to!). Believe it or not, some student loan consolidations don't even require a check of your credit history.

CHEAP$KATE

The advantages of a consolidation loan include the convenience of having only one payment (instead of several), possible savings from getting a lower interest rate, and no prepayment penalties or fees. However, make sure to watch out for higher interest rates and/or any tax implications that may be associated with getting a consolidation loan. It's not *always* the way to go, but often times it is—so look into it!

What About State Loans?

You could look around for quite a while and not locate any loans funded by state government, though there are some out there. They just seem to be few and far between. Your best bet for locating information on state loans for college students would be at the Web sites of your state's higher education agencies. A Web search for your state government's main information site or a glance at the blue pages of your telephone book (where you can find the listing for any government office) should set you in the right direction. Good luck, this could be a tricky search—but it might be worth it.

Home Equity Loans

In recent years, students and parents have been able to enjoy many tax benefits related to their educational and college loans. In addition, parents who own their homes have discovered some attractive tax advantages in taking out a home equity loan. A home equity line of credit is somewhat more flexible than other kinds of loans, though it often comes with a slightly higher interest rate. The loan is for a specific monetary amount based upon the equity in your home. You draw from a line of credit as you need the money, without having to pay interest until you receive the funds. The interest paid on equity loans can possibly be deducted on the borrower's federal tax return.

Whether or not this is a good option for your family is too complicated a question to be discussed here. Since every individual's income tax situation is unique, you should consult your personal tax preparation firm or a loan consultant for more detailed information regarding the risks and benefits of taking out a home equity loan for the purposes of paying college education expenses.

Here's a final note on borrowing money: Be conservative! Do not use loans as a substitute for scholarships, grants, student employment, or lower-interest federal loans simply because you do not want to bother with the FAFSA application or other tedious paperwork. Borrow only as much as you truly *need* for each academic year.

WHERE SHOULD THOSE BILLS GO?

In order to avoid a sticky, and serious, situation on graduation day, your family should talk about the reality of paying back loans! Before you even apply for one, it is very important that your family decides exactly who (student, mother, father, or another relative) will do the borrowing and who exactly will do the paying back.

Repayment responsibility depends on your family's private beliefs. Some families believe that it is the parents who should fulfill their obligation to pay as much as possible toward their children's higher educations. If you share this opinion, your ability to carry the financial burden may mean you have to take out one or more parent loans. Of course, not all people agree with this particular point of view. Plenty of families consider it the student's responsibility to borrow college money, if any loans are needed at all.

CHEAP$KATE

You get a bit of a break before you have to pay back your loans if you are a student borrower. The grace period lasts somewhere between six and nine months after you have graduated or have ceased to be enrolled as at least a half-time student. If you are a parent borrower, payments are usually expected to begin shortly after your loan has been fully disbursed.

Of course, there is no rule that says the responsibility of paying for college should fall solely upon any one individual's shoulders. Many families have begun to compromise too and combine the financial responsibility of paying for a college education. Some parents take out a set portion of their student's educational costs each year in parent loan money. At the same time, the student also borrows a portion of the needed funds to ease the financial burden on the parents. Whatever your family decides to do, the most important thing is to be open with each other and communicate doubts, concerns, and questions!

Chapter 8

GETTING DOUGH DURING SCHOOL

S ure, everyone wants to enter college with money for tuition, money for food, and coast through higher education with ease. But let's get serious. Even with grants, loans, and planning, reality sometimes bites! If you find yourself without money, there is one surefire way to get some, quick—get a job! That's right. Plenty of students are getting their college educations the old-fashioned way, by working their way through school. If they can do it, so can you—and there are a ton of incredible opportunities out there, if you just know where to look.

WORK WHILE IN SCHOOL!

Take a look around your college campus. You will probably see buildings everywhere. Labs, libraries, gyms, and many more—and think about it, don't most of these buildings employ students? In fact, a lot of the campus facilities are dependent upon student workers to keep the buildings open in the evening hours and over the weekends. As far as the university is concerned, student employees are a big necessity in order for the campus to continue running smoothly and economically from one day to the next. What does this mean to you? Lots of jobs, that's what. And they're probably within walking distance!

Work Is Good for You

As you've probably been hearing since you were a kid, work hard and you will see results. As a student, it's no different. When you work for your cash, you'll reap personal benefits from working on campus as well as a monetary payoff. In fact, statistics indicate that college students who work (in on- or off-campus jobs) do better in their college careers and often have higher GPAs than those who do not work at all. Other benefits of on-campus student employment include the opportunity to build business/academic contacts for the future, improved confidence, and improved time management and organization skills.

Before being hired to a particular position, students should consider any commitments they have before taking that job. No more than ten hours a week should be scheduled for work until the student gets a sense of what their class and extracurricular commitments are going to be like for the semester.

Aren't All On-Campus Jobs Boring and Minimum Wage?

Is this what you're thinking? Don't be so negative! There are a number of reasons why an on-campus job is better for students. For starters, you won't pay as much for transportation, and it won't take you a lot time to get to and from work. Jobs range from clerical and customer service positions, such as a wide variety of library positions, to jobs with professors around the campus. Students are encouraged to seek jobs in their interest areas, giving them an opportunity to gain experience within a field. The best way to find work is by contacting faculty within the department of interest. If you are interested in physics, you should contact the physics faculty and see about finding a research job. Any college's career services center can help students locate work on campus.

Even though many of the jobs are minimum wage, the upside to having an on-campus job is more than enough to make you forget about the downside. Even if your starting pay is low, by coming back to the same job year after year you are likely to earn a raise. (It would probably be a big plus if you didn't have to look for a job again next year, too.)

The biggest of the upsides is that you are better
equipped to handle scheduling work around your classes.
Off-campus jobs often require shifts of more than six
hours in a row, whereas on-campus jobs can be scheduled
for as little as those two hours between your morning
classes.

Undoubtedly, the best part is that you'll never get
stuck working on a holiday! On-campus student employees do not have to work on holidays when the university
is closed! And working during exam week? No problem.
On-campus student employees also get to have days off
during the days of exam week. Your boss at an off-campus
job likely isn't going to care much about your exams; all he
wants is for you to show up at work as usual.

GRANT-FUNDED POSITIONS

Think of a job in a federal work-study program as a self-
help way of getting financial aid. Why self-help? Because
it's all up to you! This means that you have to do some
work in order to receive the aid. Loans are also considered self-help because you have to get a job later in order
to pay the money back. In the case of federal work-study,

students must work in order to receive a paycheck. Federal work-study is a campus-based program, which means that individual schools receive a certain amount of government funds and are then able to decide how they wish to distribute those taxpayer dollars. Institutions of higher education are also required to contribute a certain percentage of their own funds to the working student's wages.

Work-Study Job Options

The jobs that are made available through the federal work-study program must be used to benefit students who have a demonstrated financial need. And there are a lot of jobs available through school's work-study programs! And they aren't all boring! A wide variety of jobs is usually available, from office worker to research assistant to computer tutor, for example. Ideally, the job should be relevant to the student's academic area of study.

These jobs, while commonly located on the college campus, also have the potential to end up being off campus. Typically, if the work-study job is performed off campus, then it will probably be at a local nonprofit agency that has an affiliation with the school. Schools are required to pay out at least minimum wage to work-study students, and they must do so at least once per month in this program.

SAVVY STUDENTS SAVE

Pay close attention to how much you have earned throughout the academic year. You may have to stop working when you have reached your limit if your institution cannot or will not increase your maximum earnings ceiling.

Getting Paid

Jobs for undergraduate students are required to pay hourly wages—not salaried. What does this mean? You will be awarded a certain dollar amount of federal work-study money as part of your financial aid package, and you cannot exceed that maximum earnings amount for the academic year and this is all based on the amount of hours you work in a day, week, month or other increment of time. In other words, be careful not to work too much because they are only allowed to pay you a certain amount!

Undergraduate work-study students often receive their money in the form of a paycheck, the amount of which depends on how many on-the-clock hours they actually worked. Direct deposit to either a checking or savings account is usually possible upon request. Graduate students may be paid hourly as well, but they also have the option of getting a salary through this program.

INTERNSHIPS—GOOD FOR NOW AND LATER!

It seems like all do-gooder students are getting internships these days. This is based on the theory that an education plus job experience prepares a student for the real-world job market. And it's true—good jobs after graduation are hard to come by, and those students who have a strong education and experience in their fields certainly have an advantage. One way students are getting the work experience they need is through internships. Some academic programs even require that students in the program complete an internship as part of the graduation requirements.

Are Interns Paid?

Let's say you want to (or, sometimes, you have to) do an internship, so let's take a closer look at what this really means. Internships can be paid or unpaid, for academic credit or not. As you investigate your internship possibilities, it is possible to find one that pays money, so always look for this option first. Start looking early—if you need a summer internship, start looking during the fall semester. Start by applying only for those internships that pay money.

Finding Opportunities

Most colleges and universities have an internship or career services office. That's a good place to start investigating internship options. Academic departments and area businesses might also have internship possibilities that aren't advertised through the college internship office. Take the initiative to stop by and find out. Professors and advisers can also help you by suggesting something based on your academic interests. Use all your resources!

In addition, the U.S. State Department and other federal agencies in the United States offer internships (most of which are unpaid) to undergraduate and graduate students. Applications for these are due each year by November 1 for summer internships, March 1 for fall, and July 1 for winter. State and city governments have many internship possibilities that often get overlooked. Jobs that require working with members of congress or state government are also available through governmental internships.

What to Do When Internships Do Not Pay

If you are required to take an internship that does not offer monetary compensation, you may want to inquire at your institution's financial aid office, dean's office, and/or career or internship office to see if there are grants or cash stipends available. You may not be able to get much of anything, but a little money is better than none. With a small stipend you may be able to at least afford to get some of your resulting internship expenses covered.

Find the Internship That Is Right for You!

There are more internships in this world than we could ever possibly hope to list here. However, just because there are so many of them does not mean that they are easy to get. In fact, there are probably more students trying to get internships than there are internships in existence. Therefore, a competitive attitude is often a key attribute for those hoping to secure an internship— paid or otherwise. The best way to fight an enemy is to first know your enemy, so the following sections provide a few examples of the kinds of high-profile internships available in the modern workforce.

Is the State Department for You?

A U.S. State Department internship is an impressive way to explore a career in diplomatic relations. Most of them are unpaid; however, unlike a lot of other internships, free housing is usually provided. To be eligible for these internships, applicants must be U.S. citizens who are undergraduates or graduate students who plan to continue on with their education until they have actually graduated. You can apply for these internships online via the State Department's Web site. For more information on federal student job opportunities, visit the U.S. government's student job Web site at *www.studentjobs.gov*.

Join the Peace Corps

The U.S. Peace Corps offers quite possibly some of the best and highest-paying entry-level intern jobs for anyone interested in humanitarian work in foreign locations. Unlike the state department jobs mentioned earlier, you will not be rubbing elbows with people in high places. The Peace Corps expects a lot of you. This means getting your hands dirty by living and working with the native peoples of your assigned region. To be eligible, applicants must be U.S. citizens.

Most Peace Corps work is meant for people with a bachelor's degree and requires a two-year commitment. However, there are exceptions with certain intern positions. Despite your position or internship, the Peace Corps pays for all of your expenses plus an additional stipend of as much as $6,000 for resettlement costs at the end of your service.

Training and support is provided to you, not to mention invaluable life experience. Educational loans can often be deferred, and some may even be partially canceled should you decide to join the Peace Corps for a full two-year term. Tuition support is also available for graduate students. Contact the Peace Corps for more information, or check *www.peacecorps.gov.*

SAVVY STUDENTS SAVE

Some study-abroad programs offer an internship option. If you are lucky enough to find an opportunity that fits your interests and academic background, you may enrich your travel with some actual international job experience. This may not pay money, but if it gives you an advantage over your peers in the job market later, it might be worthwhile, especially if you were planning to travel abroad anyway.

The Woodrow Wilson Foundation

The Woodrow Wilson Foundation hosts a number of internship programs that are related to U.S. government agencies. These internships especially encourage women and ethnic minorities to apply. Most of these

142

internships, including those for the summer, come with scholarships that are enough to fund several years of study. Applicants must apply before the end of their sophomore year to be eligible for three-year scholarship awards or before the end of their senior year to be eligible for graduate school scholarships (which are good for a significantly shorter length of time).

Private Sector Internships

Many international internship programs are sponsored by big business institutions and corporations, such as Procter & Gamble, Coca-Cola, the Altria Group, and Microsoft, among others. These are sometimes restricted exclusively to students whose goal is to enter an MBA program. In other words, if you want to get one of these internships, it really helps to be a business major. Majors in the liberal arts have countless options in business and government sectors also. Most businesses and government agencies list their internship possibilities on their Web sites under their employment/career links.

Many undergraduate students take advantage of overseas internships with host-country companies. Most of these internships with private sector companies only pay their interns enough of a salary to cover their basic living expenses—which, you should note, does not include the cost of overseas airfare. Do a Web search to find companies offering these internships, using the corporation's name, the word "internship," and your chosen country as search words. There's nothing wrong with contacting a company that you are interested in and suggesting that they start an internship program too!

GET CREATIVE!

Are you one of those people who made lemonade stands and sold rocks as a child? Do you consider yourself an entrepreneur? It's true, not everybody travels the straight and narrow path when it comes to finding a source of income. In fact, there are those among us who do not travel on a defined path at all. If you refuse to choose security over creativity, and are ready and willing to take risks, this section is for you. You have a number of possible options—some are just a little more "unorthodox" than others.

Do you have a particular hobby that you really enjoy? Do you love working with your hands in the garden or know how to care for animals? Are you a talented ballet dancer? You might wish you could be spending more of your time developing your favorite hobby and less time working at a job that just does not excite you (or that you hate with all your heart). Believe it or not, you may not have to choose between your hobby and a paycheck. It might be easier than you think for you to go to work and enjoy your hobby at the same time.

Know What You're Getting Into!

When you start thinking about turning your favorite hobby into a source of income, don't forget to do your homework. Get the facts before you venture out because, sorry to break it to you, even though you might have enjoyed training your puppy to sit and shake hands, you might not be cut out to be a pro dog trainer.

The first step is to research the market thoroughly. There may be obstacles along the way that could mean big trouble for you if you're not careful. Whether you plan to start your own full-fledged business, or spend a few hours a week earning a little extra spending money, find out the laws and regulations that apply to you before you start posting flyers.

Different states have varying kinds of licenses for different kinds of jobs. Being your own boss sounds fun—but come tax-time, you may find yourself dishing out even more money to the federal government. As a self-employed person, you must pay the full portion of Social Security taxes (as an employee, you can count on your employer to kick in half). This, plus other taxes and the general cost of doing business, can turn what looked like an easy profit into money and effort down the drain.

CHEAP$KATE

Consignment shops are a great way to sell anything from handmade clothing to artwork such as sketches, sculptures, and paintings. Consignment shops will display your self-made products in a sales environment and pay you for each item of yours that they sell.

Attitude Adjustment

Successful entrepreneurs are enthusiastic about their ideas and dedicated to their businesses. This sounds simple enough, but it can be a lot tougher when it actually comes down to doing it. To be an entrepreneur, you cannot be the kind of person who has dozens of hobbies and likes to do a little of this and that, here and there, without ever truly committing to any major passion. You must not allow yourself to be distracted, abandoning an idea during development to give attention to the next idea that captures your interest. Successful entrepreneurs are generally committed to perfection and dedicated to achieving their goals. They know how to get going when the going gets tough. These are the people who are successful—the ones who actually *make* money!

SAVVY STUDENTS SAVE

If you do consider yourself the entrepreneurial type, it might be a good idea to take a course or two in business, no matter what your major is. Coming up with ideas will help you put a business together, but it is the little details of the business world that can soon bring your "good idea" crashing to the ground before it has even had a chance to take off.

Start a Business

Not all enthusiastic and dedicated people turn out to be great entrepreneurs, but optimism is essential to even get your idea off the ground. Whether you are the owner of the local news rag or the CEO of a *Fortune* 500 crew, you must be able to see positive opportunities in difficult or negative situations. Without a certain level of optimism, it will prove nearly impossible to motivate your workers, or to keep your business moving whenever times get hard (and, eventually, they will). So consider this, is your wallet half full or half empty?

Do What You Love

What are your hobbies, passions, and interests? Do you have any specialized skills? What inspires you? What gets you motivated?

146

Running a business is like studying for hours and hours for a test and then finally taking it. You may be scared when the test starts. You might be happy and enthusiastic at certain times during the test, and moody or doubtful when you encounter other questions. And there are going to be times when it is going to be tough! (They don't call it a "test" because it's a walk in the park!) However, there is no going halfway—you are either in or you aren't. Decide before you begin. Being an entrepreneur means having the responsibility to ensure that your business develops and grows until it is able to function without your constant supervision, attention, and intervention. You've got to decide how the business will operate, as well as find a way to control your operations while overseeing them.

Friends Do Not Let Friends Become Their Employees

It is imperative to any small business, or any business for that matter, that the right people are hired to do the right kinds of jobs. Your friend who goes on impulse shopping sprees with credit cards her parents do not even realize she has yet may not be a good choice for a business partner. Certainly don't make her your chief financial officer. Oh, and you know that friend whose back seat is so full trash that nobody can sit back there? He would not exactly be a great candidate for records keeper.

If you have responsible friends who want to get involved, by all means, let them help. But make sure you spell out your requirements and expectations clearly beforehand. If you are the boss, make that clear too! Both parties must be able to keep in mind that this is a business proposition, and that during business hours, you're employer and employee and not best buddies. You're going to do what's best for your business and your employees need to know that you might have to fire them if they aren't performing.

CHEAP$KATE

Consider all possible tax benefits if you have a small business. Write off everything you can to lessen the amount of tax paid. That will free up more dollars for more important things, like your education!

Have a Plan!

Sometimes it's hard to confront your fears and make decisions. Decisions mean commitment. Bad decisions lead to problems and can mean losing the respect of one's peers. Owning a business—particularly an undercapitalized startup—is all about making decisions with limited market research and imperfect information. Where should your business be located? Can you do it from your room? Do you need to hire help? How should you price your products? What should be your first target market? One of the main differences between having a hobby and having a business is the need to make real decisions with financial implications. Will you enjoy it?

It Takes Money to Make Money

Again, depending on your hobbies, passions, and interests, you may need to create a business plan and generate some cash to get started. Once you've written a business plan and established that your hobby can indeed be a sustainable business, the next step is to finance its execution. Unless you thrive on adversity, do not quit your day job (or in your case, college) until you know that you have sufficient money to fund your business plan. Getting financing is not easy and requires personal sacrifice— whether it involves borrowing from your family's savings, your relatives and friends, credit cards, or professional investors. If things do not work out exactly as mapped out in your business plan, will you be able to support a contingency plan to ensure that the business survives? If you do not have the money from your personal network, will you be willing to sacrifice ownership and control to outside investors? Obviously, starting your own full-fledged business is a lot of work. If this sounds like more than you're up for right now, don't be discouraged. There are still plenty of ways you can make money.

CHEAP$KATE

Remember that there is absolutely nothing wrong with any job that you finally choose to do, as long as it comes with a paycheck. College is not the time to find your dream job; it is the time to get the education that you need in order to find a dream job *after* you have graduated.

Chapter 9

REPORTING TO DUTY! GET MONEY FOR YOUR SERVICE

If it's high school graduation time and you still don't know what you're doing about college, you're in trouble now, mister or miss! None of your money has been saved? A Section 529 plan is wishful thinking at this point. You don't have the grades to get a good scholarship or enough demonstrated financial need to be awarded aid. Welcome to America, my friend! Luckily, we live in a country where with a few years of military service, you can completely pay for your education (with enough left over each semester to help pay living expenses).

THE MONTGOMERY GI BILL

The GI Bill was first signed into law by Franklin D. Roosevelt on June 22, 1944. In 1984, former Mississippi Governor Sonny Montgomery modified the GI Bill to what it is now. Today, the "Montgomery" GI Bill provides many benefits, including educational ones, to enlisted military personnel from the moment they head for boot camp or basic training. Surprisingly, the U.S. government does not try to hide the fact that this money is available. In fact, signing up for the GI Bill is actively encouraged. Even if, as a member of our armed forces, you were to opt out during boot camp processing and choose not to sign up, eventually one of your superior officers would probably insist that you get with the program.

Stay Ahead of the Game

If you are male and were born on or after January 1, 1960, and are not currently serving active duty in the U.S. armed forces, you must register with the Selective Service in order to receive federal financial aid. This is easy to do when you complete the FAFSA. Just check "Yes" to the question, "If you are male (age 18–25) and not registered, answer Yes and Selective Service will register you."

This is not because your participation benefits them in any way. They've just seen what happens to those who separate from the military without the GI Bill. With no way to pay for school, a lot of former military members who opted out of the GI Bill are left with no other option but to work in low or minimum wage jobs, with little hope of ever improving their vocation. (And many of them end up right back in the military in only a few short years—when it was never in their plans to become a career soldier).

How the GI Bill Works

First of all, you should know that the GI Bill is not exactly free money. You do have to work for it. You must have served in Active Duty or be a member of the Selected Reserve to qualify. The Montgomery GI Bill—Active Duty, or MGIB, provides up to thirty-six months of financial assistance to eligible veterans. The education benefits can be used for a wide variety of educational programs including college, technical or vocational schools, flight training, and correspondence courses. The Montgomery GI Bill—Selected Reserve program is similar, except it is for members of the Army Reserve, Navy Reserve, Air Force Reserve, Marine Corps Reserve, Coast Guard Reserve, Army National Guard, and the Air National Guard. Similar to the active duty program, the education benefits can be used for a wide variety of coursework. To qualify for either of these Montgomery GI Bill programs, you must have completed (or in some cases currently be fulfilling) a service obligation. Three years (or more) of service seems like a lot. However, when you stop to think of exactly what you end up getting in return for that commitment, it seems a little crazy not to take the deal.

What It's Worth

On average, the GI Bill is worth about $20,000 for college. You get this benefit in exchange for a four-year stint in whatever branch of service you choose and a minimal deduction from your military pay. Think about that.

If you join the military but choose not to take advantage of the GI Bill, it would be similar to turning down a legitimate, federally endorsed deal for a payoff of $20,000 in exchange for about a $1,200 investment (spread out in twenty-four easy biweekly payments over the span of a year). Think about it: How smart is it to say no to a deal that can only benefit you?

Who Is Eligible?

The Active Duty version of the GI Bill requires veterans to have an honorable discharge, a high school diploma or GED, and in some cases, at least twelve hours of college credit. In addition, veterans must meet the requirements of one of four different categories to qualify for MGIB benefits:

Category I

Entered active duty for the first time after June 30, 1985

Had military pay reduced by $100/month for first 12 months

Continuously served for 3 years, or 2 years if that is what you first enlisted for, or 2 years if you entered the Selected Reserve within one year of leaving active duty and served 4 years ("2 x 4" program)

Category II

Entered active duty before January 1, 1977

Served at least 1 day between 10/19/84 and 6/30/85, and stayed on active duty through 6/30/88 (or

6/30/87 if you entered the Selected Reserve within 1 year of leaving active duty and served 4 years)

On 12/31/89, you had entitlement left from the Vietnam-Era GI Bill

Category III

Not eligible for MGIB under Category I or II

On active duty on 9/30/90 and separated involuntarily after 2/2/91

or involuntarily separated on or after 11/30/93

or voluntarily separated under either the Voluntary Separation Incentive (VSI) or Special Separation Benefit (SSB) program

Before separation, you had military pay reduced by $1,200

Category IV

On active duty on 10/9/96 and you had money remaining in a VEAP account on that date and you elected MGIB by 10/9/97

Or entered full-time National Guard duty under title 32, USC, between 7/1/85, 11/28/89 and you elected MGIB during the period 10/9/96 through 7/8/97

Had military pay reduced by $100/month for 12 months or made a $1,200 lump-sum contribution

Note: Information from Department of Veterans Affairs Web site.

ENROLL TODAY AND GET AFFORDABLE SCHOOLING LATER

Although all of the armed services offer the GI Bill, the army has gotten especially enthusiastic about their educational benefits over the last ten years—it's true, the lure of big bucks for tuition is one heck of a recruitment hook for soon-to-be high school graduates. It was in the spirit of such enthusiasm that the army gave birth to the Concurrent Admissions Program, or ConAP. ConAP is a joint agreement between the army and more than 1,800 community colleges, vocational schools, and four-year institutions across the country. The goal of this program is to increase enlistment of active-duty and reserve soldiers in general, and the number of soldiers, veterans, and reservists enrolled in college.

SAVVY STUDENTS SAVE

A group of participating colleges offers army soldiers the opportunity to complete a college degree and/or vocational certificate online at any given time, as long as they're stationed at a military installation that hosts this program.

The ConAP program allows people to enlist in the army while stating their intentions to enroll in college during and/or after their term of enlistment. This statement of intent is made at the same time they sign up for duty. This stated intention to enroll is then deferred for up to two years after a soldier is given honorable discharge.

156

The U.S. Army and participating colleges maintain contact with ConAP soldiers in order to encourage off-duty study and to help these soldiers become familiar with how the ConAP program works. For more information on the ConAP program, including answers to frequently asked questions, visit the Concurrent Admissions Program for Army Enlistees Web site.

More about the Enigma Called MGIB

As a discharged GI Bill carrier, before you can receive a monthly check, you must already be enrolled in and attending college courses. The difficulty here is that if you do not find some way to pay for your classes before they start, the school will void your enrollment in a heartbeat (or so the policies often state), making the GI Bill benefits void in the process. Although it may seem confusing, the truth is, the program *is* set up to serve you. It just takes a little investigational effort to figure out how to work the system, or at least how to make that system work for you.

Working the System

Most schools offer some form of short-term or emergency loans, which postpone the payment of tuition by shifting numbers around and paying the tuition for you—based, of course, on the understanding that you will pay that money back in full, including interest and fees. This will cover you until your GI Bill check comes through, and you can use that money to pay back the loan you took from your school.

When completing the FAFSA, you must list the value of your veteran's educational benefits and the number of months during the academic year (July 1 through June 30) in which you will receive them. This information is not used in calculating your expected family contribution. However, federal regulations require that these benefits be counted as part of your financial aid package.

On the first day of the month after you have started attending classes, you will need to verify your enrollment either online (at *www.va.gov*) or over the phone. Many people find that the phone verification is much easier than the online process. You can confirm your enrollment status or handle other matters related to your benefits by calling the Veteran's Affairs Office at (877) 823-2378. In terms of actual minutes, the phone verification is usually faster (and the call is toll free). Listen carefully to the automated menu, and enter your information exactly as it is requested.

Once your call is complete, your enrollment is verified for the month (and the recording tells you what month you are verified for). You should receive your check in seven to ten days (as the recording also makes clear). If you have arranged to receive your GI Bill by direct deposit (with the funds electronically deposited directly into your bank account), the funds will probably be deposited in about seven days. Direct deposit is the fastest way to get your funds and means you don't have to wait those extra three days for a check (which often comes at the last minute).

YOU GET WHAT YOU GIVE

Just because you have the GI Bill does not mean that your benefits will be equal to another veteran's benefits. This is because the benefits are based on your time in service and what kind of service that was. Were you on active duty or were you a reservist? Were you in for two years or for four? Did you opt to pay out more money for the GI Bill while in service? All of these factors have an effect on how much you get. However, the bottom line is that you will get money for college—guaranteed.

Stay Ahead of the Game

In December of 2003, as part of the HEROES Act, the U.S. Department of Education changed some of the requirements for federal student aid programs that active-duty military personnel must meet. An example of such a modification is the extension of a student's allowed grace period before he or she starts making repayment of student loans. Under the HEROES Act, rather than the standard six to nine months, the grace period can be up to three years. Individuals should work with their lender to determine the grace period for their specific situation.

Veterans who were on active duty receive more money and enjoy more benefits than reservists usually do. Why? It is a matter of investment returns as far as the government and its tax-paying citizens are concerned. We spend the same amount of money on the initial training of an active-duty soldier as on a reservist. However, we receive more work in return from the active-duty service member. The greater return provided on our investment earns that service member access to an increased range of benefits.

Here is an example of the educational assistance allowance benefits for active duty terms of service:

- Minimum three-year enlistment = total benefit of $38,700 for college (paid out at approximately $1,075 per month for thirty-six academic months, if enrolled full time)

Once your full enlistment has been served, you can leave the military and draw your GI Bill benefits to go back to school.

Tell Me More about Reserve Duty

Reservists do not earn as much in educational benefits as a soldier who has served on active duty, though they do receive college benefits. For example, army reservists can earn more than $10,000 for college in a snap. However, there is just one catch—they have to enlist for no less than a term of six years. The current monthly benefit is up to $309 for full-time enrollment.

To qualify for the Montgomery GI Bill Selected Reserve, you must meet the following requirements:

- Have a six-year obligation to serve in the Selected Reserve signed after June 30, 1985. If you are an officer, you must have agreed to serve six years in addition to your original obligation. For some types of training, it is necessary to have a six-year commitment that begins after September 30, 1990.
- Complete your initial active duty for training (IADT).

- Meet the requirement to receive a high school diploma or equivalency certificate before completing IADT. You may not use 12 hours toward a college degree to meet this requirement.
- Remain in good standing while serving in an active Selected Reserve unit.
Note: Information from Department of Veterans Affairs Web site.

Maybe the disparity in benefits seems unfair. The army reserve makes a good-hearted attempt to make that up to you. They will even help you earn more money for college. However, once again there is a catch—you have to be assigned to critical skill positions or critical units. Such assignments can increase the benefits for a reservist to over $22,000.

Stay Ahead of the Game

Be sure to inform your institution's financial aid office if your status with the military changes, especially if you have been called up to active duty. It is essential for the financial aid office to be made aware of your situation so that administrators can take the necessary steps to preserve your financial aid status so you still have your benefits when you return.

The army reserve calls such a program a GI Bill "kicker." Depending on your occupational specialty and what unit you are assigned to during a critical assignment, your "kicker" could mean an extra $100 to $350 a month for full-time attendance. This may not sound like much to you now, but when you're in school and the bills start piling up, that extra money each month will be more than welcome.

Your Education Benefits—
Where Do You Wanna Go?

You are not restricted to a traditional four-year university in order to get an education using the GI Bill. The GI Bill is intended to help veterans find a vocational skill that will allow them to enter the civilian workforce productively, and not all occupations require a four-year degree. Just about any kind of training or educational course you take for the purpose of finding or improving your vocational skills can be eligible for GI Bill endorsement. Degree and technical certificate programs are just one example. Other possibilities include flight training, apprenticeships, on-the-job-training, and certain kinds of correspondence courses.

SAVVY STUDENTS SAVE

Members of the military should keep a hard copy file of their leave and earnings statements (LES), even after receiving their honorable discharge/separation papers. These records may help you to answer questions on the FASFA should you need to file for financial aid immediately after your discharge.

NICKELS AND DIMES AND THE NATIONAL GUARD

The "selected reserve" category includes reserves for all branches of the U.S. Armed Forces: Army, Navy, Air Force, Marine Corps, and Coast Guard, as well as the Army National Guard and the Air National Guard. What does this mean? It means there's not a lick of difference between the GI Bill benefits offered to reservists and national guardsmen. Money shouldn't be a factor if you happen to find yourself torn between these two options.

The GI Bill still provides national guardsmen with as much as thirty-six months of tuition benefits for the purposes of college, vocational courses, business classes, and certain correspondence courses. However, national guardsmen (unlike reservists) are restricted by tighter rules concerning what courses they're allowed to take. Some courses of study that are available to reservists are not endorsed for national guardsmen.

BENEFITS GALORE

Feeling gung-ho yet? Well, the fun is just beginning, because your military training, courses, and occupational specialty can all count for college credit. Another bonus to National Guard service is that every state has some sort of additional education benefit for its members. This is in addition to any federal educational benefits received through the Montgomery GI Bill for Selected Reserves. Generally, the state educational programs can be used at the same time as the Montgomery GI Bill. The good news is that many states offer at least $1,000 per semester in additional tuition benefit and some states will kick in up to 100 percent of tuition. The bad news is that benefits may actually be less if state budget funds run out in a given year.

Receiving College Credit

Policies vary from one college to another, and they can also change depending on the program of study you have chosen. When you contact a school, have your paperwork on hand. If you are a discharged vet, you will need to dig up your DD-214 forms (those are the papers they handed you and said not to lose when you were discharged). If you no longer know where to find your DD-214, you will need to complete a form called an SF 180 in order to verify your military transcript.

Not all military training courses appear on a military transcript, so keep track of the records for all the classes you have taken for military training. Look over your military transcript to be sure it is still accurate. In certain extreme cases, as many as five or more years of military experience can qualify for several full-time semesters' worth of college credit.

When requesting a transcript to be sent to your school, it should be sent directly from the transcript office to the school (not to you and then the school). However, you should also request an unofficial transcript for your review. Request this personal copy before you request the transcript that's going to be sent to the school administrators. That way, you can have any necessary corrections made. Remember that each branch of service has its own unique transcript request forms and process. Know which you are using, and be sure it is correct.

SAVVY STUDENTS SAVE

All veterans should consult their local veteran's administration office—almost all college campuses have one—to find out about their specific benefits. Selected reservists should also be aware of the fact that their entitlements under the GI Bill will permanently expire fourteen years from the date that they became eligible for the program or from the date that they left their branch of the selected reserve.

A Foot in the Door

Joining the military can be a lot like joining an exclusive club. For members of the Marine Corps this rings especially true. They are more fanatical about brotherhood than a college fraternity. Such camaraderie can be a great advantage when you finally get your walking papers and enter the civilian world. Many human resource administrators are on the lookout for military veterans with good records and honorable discharges. (You may find that many administrators have served time in the military themselves.) That piece of information on your resume alone is sometimes enough to get you an interview when you might otherwise not have gotten so much as a form letter.

JROTC—START IN HIGH SCHOOL

Junior ROTC leadership education develops good citizenship, self-confidence, and self-discipline. Leadership classes introduce cadets to training elements such as leadership, military customs, drill and ceremonies, uniform inspections, physical fitness training, marksmanship, and Marine Corps history. Cadets are required to participate in civic service, wear a uniform, and dress up in nice civilian clothes at least twice a month. Joining JROTC while in high school can help you become eligible for a number of scholarships.

ROTC

The Reserve Officer's Training Corps, or ROTC, is a program for college students who intend to become officers in the military after graduating. (This is not the same as JROTC, which is for high school students.) This is not an umbrella program, and the requirements for eligibility may change from one branch of the service to another. Anyone who is interested in ROTC participation should be sure that they know what they are getting themselves into before signing anything. For example, the Marine Corps requires that every marine go to boot camp, while other branches of service count officer training as a boot camp equivalent. Some ROTC programs count your military science education while in college as "basic training."

Stay Ahead of the Game

To get a jump-start on a military career, and improve your odds of getting accepted into an ROTC program, you may want to join a military program while you're still in high school. Programs like JROTC, the Naval Sea Cadet Corps, and the Civil Air Patrol are all open to high school students. They will give anyone looking at a future in the military a nice jump on the competition.

JROTC Order of Daedalian Scholarships

The Order of Daedalians honors all World War I aviators who were commissioned as officers and as military pilots before the 1918 armistice. These pilots were the first to fly airplanes in wartime. The organization funds a comprehensive awards program, supports the military services, and donates funds to other aerospace and flight-related activities. It is intended to foster patriotism while encouraging good character and integrity in young Americans. The Daedalian Foundation's scholarship program also promotes JROTC students with a focus of study in aerospace disciplines.

Some examples of military scholarship programs are:

The Reserve Officer Training Corps (ROTC)

Air Force Reserve Officer Training Corps (AFROTC)

Naval Reserve Officers Training Corps (NROTC, for both the Navy and Marine Corps).

Daedalian JROTC Awards Offered

There is a veritable gold mine of scholarship awards available to high school students participating in the JROTC program. No matter what branch of JROTC you participate in, there is a scholarship that you are eligible for. Let's take a look at a number of these JROTC exclusive scholarships:

- The Daedalian JROTC Achievement Award is presented each year to outstanding third-year cadets who are attending one of the participating high schools.
- Begun in 1978, the Daedalian Matching Scholarship Program is an annual cash award, given to match flight scholarships that are given to worthy students with a strong desire to become military pilots.
- The Major General Lucas V. Beau Flight Scholarship is another award from the Daedalian Order. It is announced each year to Civil Air Patrol cadets who demonstrate a desire for military careers in aviation and who use the Civil Air Patrol for ground and flight training leading to a private pilot's license.

- Daedalian Air Force ROTC Scholarships are awarded yearly to Air Force ROTC cadets who have performed in an outstanding manner.
- The Daedalian Army ROTC Scholarships are awarded annually to the previous year's outstanding nonscholarship MS-IV Aviation Branch ROTC cadets.
- The Daedalian Naval ROTC Scholarships are presented yearly to senior naval ROTC cadets who possess the desire and capability to become future naval aviators.
- The Daedalian Foundation Descendants Scholarship Program offers a number of cash scholarships for the study of aerospace engineering and flight and is awarded annually to descendants of members of the Daedalian Order.
- The Daedalian Colonel Charles Getchell Memorial Scholarships consist of five awards presented each year to outstanding ROTC cadets. This program was made possible by a donation from Mrs. Getchell, widow of founder Colonel Charles Getchell.

SAVVY STUDENTS SAVE

Military scholarships are awarded on the basis of physical, humanitarian, or academic merit, and not on financial need. After graduating from college, recipients are usually required to serve in a branch of the U.S. Armed Forces for a set number of years.

How JROTC Benefits You?

If you have at least two years of active membership in any JROTC-related, paramilitary program, it can mean good things for you when and if you decide that the military route is for you. If you have two years of membership, you may enter military service with an automatic promotion to E-2, one step up in the enlisted ranks from E-1, where everyone else is at the beginning (not a big jump up the chain, but it's at least a start). Your years of JROTC participation must be consecutive, and they must also be in the same branch of JROTC.

Chapter 10

TAKE ADVANTAGE OF THE FREE STUFF

Y ou might be surprised when you learn how much free and discounted stuff there is out there! From the smallest school supplies to larger items for the dorm room, it's not a question of "are they out there?" it's "where and how do I get them?" You might have to be a bit aggressive and sometimes you might have to change the way you think about things, but here you will learn how to find free money for the things you really need!

SCHOOL SUPPLIES CAN ADD UP!

At first, one might think that there are few other expenses to be concerned with outside of tuition and books. However, items such as paper, pens, pencils, folders, CDs, and blue books can start to add up not long into the semester. At any exam, without failure, there will always be that one student at the classroom door who is panhandling for a blue book or even a pencil. Most people think this student is just unprepared for class. Have you ever thought that maybe this student is just broke and couldn't afford the couple of bucks it takes to pull one of each of these items together? It could be true—especially with the high prices that college bookstores often offer. Are you hoping that you don't become that student? Well, you don't have to. There are ways to save on supplies and stay prepared—you just have to know the tricks.

SAVVY STUDENTS SAVE

Shop with a friend and buy in bulk to save money. Ramen noodles cost only pennies a package when you buy a whole case. The same savings apply to school supplies. Split value packs of pens, notepads, or whatever else you need.

Do Supplies Qualify As Tax Write-Offs?

In a word, "No." In most cases, expenses for textbooks and school supplies cannot be used for tax credits such as Lifetime Learning. They are also not qualified under the new tax breaks for higher-education expenses. However, if a student is required to directly pay the institution for certain supplies, meaning that buying those items is a requirement under the student's enrollment or admission, those items would then qualify as valid tax-deductible expenses. Keep track of the expenses so that when tax season comes around you'll remember!

Around Town

Here is a universal truth—if a big name organization, company, or other group is handing out free promotional items, people are going to take them. These handouts increase a company's overhead, and its marketing department will likely request a bigger budget the following year, but smart businesspeople simply do not care. Why? Because if some moocher has a cupful of pens with that company's logo on it sitting on his or her desk, then to the businessperson, it was money well spent. Pens have a tendency to switch owners a few times before they finally make it into the wastebasket. Students always have a use for pens that still work. To the broke students, free pens can be almost as good as free food.

CHEAP$KATE

One excellent way to raise money is to hold a garage sale before you head off to school and sell the things you do not need. If you offer to pick up discarded items from relatives and friends too, you will have more to sell, and you will help them out by hauling their unwanted items away.

Are you skeptical about the truth behind the "freebie" mentality? Perhaps you think the freebie always comes with a catch. If so, answer this question—if freebies don't work as a promotional tool, then why are there so many Web sites online devoted to advertising and offering them? When a company offers free stickers at a Web site, the intention is to attract loyal site roamers to send an e-mail asking for some. The company then has another address to use when they send out e-mail advertising. Once the foolproof solidity of this idea was realized, everybody and their CEO started using "specialty advertising" freebie offers on the Web.

On the Web

To find freebies and/or freebie-specific Web sites, start by opening your favorite search engine and doing a search for "cheap free school supplies." You will immediately see just how many options there are online. This is not exactly the fastest way to locate the specific type of "freebie" that you are in search of, but it is a good way to start. Just don't get distracted by the offer for 1,000 golf tees (with Joe's Roadkill Shack advertisements on them) while you are doing your search. As you look around, anyone and everyone you run into is going to try to get you to take something and, if you like, take anything you want that's offered—so long as you do not lose sight of why you started searching in the first place.

CHEAP$KATE

Students should never miss the opportunity to get free school supplies. Many local businesses also try to attract new students as potential customers by offering things they will find useful. Take what you are given, but be sure not to sign anything resembling a contract. You might get duped into more than you bargained for.

Redistributing the Wealth

The National Association for the Exchange of Industrial Resources (NAEIR) offers assistance to supplement tight budgets for a number of nonprofit organizations by way of their somewhat unusual membership program. The group has come up with a clever way of finding supplies to redistribute to students in need by collecting donations from overstocked inventories from big and small American businesses. Over the span of a quarter century, NAEIR has pulled together and redistributed donations worth more than $1.6 billion.

Members of the NAEIR simply pick what they want from a catalog that they receive five times throughout the year. Once members make a selection, they pay for the shipping and handling costs. NAEIR members pull in an average $18,000 worth of supplies a year. However, memberships to the NAEIR are not free for everyone, and you must represent a legitimate nonprofit organization. (By the way, student organizations and clubs are considered nonprofit.)

LITTLE KNOWN BUT LIFE-SAVING HELP!

As you have already seen, the high and rising costs of college textbooks is one of the biggest financial burdens for anyone trying to acquire a higher education. However, even with textbooks, there are options that a student can choose from to help ease that burden just a little. The main way to get help comes in the form of what are called textbook vouchers. These can come from a number of different sources and can really help with minimizing cash strain.

There are often no rules forbidding students from posting flyers to sell their textbooks themselves. Hold on to
your textbooks until the next semester, and then post
them at a few dollars less than what the bookstore
is charging for the used version of that book. You are
almost guaranteed to get more for it than you would
have from the bookstore.

How to Get a Voucher

Textbook vouchers are great but there are some limitations to consider. While these vouchers are offered by a
lot of institutions and organizations, they are given only
to those students who have been approved for financial
aid, and they are accepted only during specific times of
the academic year. In some cases, the vouchers are automatically offered as part of the financial aid package for
needy students. In other cases they may be part of an academic or athletic scholarship, or they may be a completely
separate scholarship.

Once they've been awarded, textbook vouchers can
normally be obtained at the institution's campus business
office. Students who use vouchers should plan on having
about $300 or more at the beginning of the college year
for their textbooks. Student supplies such as notebooks,
pencils, computer disks, and blue books may not be pur-
chased with textbook vouchers. You don't get cash back
from a voucher purchase, and they will be accepted for
the total amount of the textbook purchase only.

Another organization, called Focus America, is a
nonprofit organization in New Jersey. It has a program
for high school and college students in which they volun-

teer thirty hours of service in exchange for a $50 textbook gift certificate. A program such as that benefits you in two ways: you can obtain volunteer work experience, which is great for your scholarship applications and resume, and you earn a voucher toward your book costs.

Refund Checks Can Be Vouchers, Too

Students who have financial assistance credit balances left over (in amounts that are sufficient to purchase textbooks) may charge those books against their credit balance. For example, let's say you had $8,000 in scholarships and financial aid allotted to you for the year, and your total tuition turned out to be around $7,500. That would leave you an extra $500. You would then be able to charge your textbooks toward that extra money. You just need to request a refund check/textbook voucher in the amount of the balance from the institution's cashiers' office. These vouchers are also sometimes available at the university bookstore. Different schools have different policies on when this money can be made available, so this option is not always convenient for everyone.

Are Vouchers Always Good for Students?

This all sounds great doesn't it? Unfortunately, there is a downside to the voucher system, mainly because it restricts the student's choices as a consumer. With a voucher, you have no choice but to get your books from the campus bookstore. So if you find a textbook for a better deal at a different bookstore, you don't have the option of paying the lower price for the book. That's because book vouchers can only be used at the university bookstore. For example, a book used for two semesters of a humanities course might cost a student $75. However, the same text is also available at an online retailer, in used but acceptable condition, for only $20. A student with a textbook voucher has no choice but to pay the $75 for a new text from the campus store or maybe $50 for a used one (if they even have any used books left). Either way, the student is not getting as much bang for a buck, voucher or no voucher.

A Computer, for Free?

If the school you decide to attend says that you *must* have a computer of your own, or if you think it is necessary to have your own, then consider investigating the college's policy regarding computer costs. A free computer? Sounds good, doesn't it? It is a very real possibility, though one that's somewhat little known and that rarely gets taken advantage of by students.

Remember that each institution creates its own budget, or total cost of attendance, for students. The cost of attendance is the maximum in financial aid that any student can receive from all available financial aid resources. That means the total package can include scholarships, grants, loans, and so on. Any of these can be used to help students buy their own personal computers. "But," you say, "don't most schools now have computer labs that are open for student use at no cost?" Yes, they do. However, please read on before dismissing the great advantage of having a computer at your own exclusive disposal.

Computer Labs Can Be a Pain

Most colleges and universities have computer labs where students who do not have their own computers can go to do assignments, write papers, check e-mail, and so on. If you walk into one of these computer labs, you are likely to see many students using the machines. This is an arrangement that works very well for a lot of students. Very few institutions actually require students to have their own computers, so do not feel that you have to make that major purchase if you are someone who does not mind using the lab computers for free. (Just remember that sometimes all of the computers are being used, and you might have to wait in line to access one.)

SAVVY STUDENTS SAVE

Some universities have begun to offer waivers of out-of-state tuition increases for students who qualify for the school's honors program. This means that a high GPA and an excellent academic record can do more than just help you get into a good college; they can also help you get money to pay for it.

Federal Regulations Can Help

Ever wondered: Can't the government do anything about the high cost of textbooks? The answer is, yes, they can! Federal regulations allow a financial aid office to add the cost of purchasing or renting a computer to your official cost of attendance. Institutions are not required to add this expense to the cost of attendance, but most will. If the institution does allow for this expense, then the cost of the computer must be documented with the financial aid office. Usually the purchase can be in the name of the student, student's spouse, or student's parent, as long as it is intended for the student's educational use.

Allowable expenses include the computer hardware, printer, and necessary software.

The government allows schools to set their own policy and maximum allowable amounts, so there is some variation in policies among institutions. One institution might allow a one-time $1,500 increase to the cost of attendance for the purchase of a computer. Another institution might allow $2,500, allowing a student to request $1,300 as an entering freshman, for example, and another $1,200 as a rising senior.

Let's take a close look at how this works: Suppose a student enrolls at a college that allows a $2,000 one-time-only computer expense, and that the institution's policy states that the purchase must be made no sooner than June (if you entered the college in August) and that receipts are required.

If you were able to borrow enough money from grandma to purchase a computer after July 1 for a cost of about $1,800, then submit the college's computer expense form, along with receipts, the college would increase your cost of attendance budget by $1,800. (You can't get more money back than the computer actually cost). This means that students are eligible to receive an extra $1,800 in financial aid.

Of course, eligibility does not mean that you will automatically receive the additional money. It just means that you now have "room" to accept that much more financial aid. If nothing else, you can at least take out a low-interest alternative student loan (and remember—pay back your grandma!).

EVEN MORE AID— TEXTBOOKS AND COMPUTERS

Federal financial aid is not the only way to get vouchers for your textbooks or money for a computer. Loans, certain scholarships, and a number of grants can and will help out with the high prices of textbooks and computers. For example, any surplus on tuition aid can more often than not be used toward your textbooks or other educational expenses. Take a look at some of the following examples. Even if you don't see anything that directly applies to your situation, ask your particular financial aid source whether there is money available that you can use toward textbooks and other supplies. There's gotta be a way that works for you!

Use Your PLUS Loan

One thing that a number of parents have begun to do is to charge the cost of their student's personal computer to their credit card, and then submit the receipts forms for the purchase(s) to be included as a part of their PLUS loan. Once the student's entire tuition bill is paid off in full for that academic year, any excess funds that have been created from the PLUS loan can then be refunded so that the parent can pay off credit card charges for the computer.

CHEAP$KATE

Some students with financial need can qualify for state programs that will lend help for the purchase of certain grocery items or other essential things. Every state's program is (of course) different, just as every student's situation is unique. If you think you might qualify and are interested in finding out what might be available, contact your local state assistance agency. It can't hurt.

Use Excess Scholarship/Grant Money

The really fortunate students who have more scholarship money and grant assistance than they know what to do with can purchase a personal computer with these excess funds. All they need to do is follow their institution's procedure for increasing the cost of attendance, then accept another scholarship or grant for up to that allowable amount. Again, you would have to find a way to pay for the computer up front (out of your own pocket), or charge it to a credit card, until they receive a refund/reimbursement check for the cost after the tuition account is paid off by the scholarship/grant funds. Now that's a great way to purchase your own personal computer without putting a permanent dent in your bank account!

Where to Ask

Every college and/or university is different. If you want a computer and don't know how to get one because you can't afford one, inquire at your college or university about their specific policy. Don't take the easy way out and glance at the Web site and think, "wow, there's nothing here, they must not offer it." More often than not, this information can be obtained face to face if you ask the right people. Colleges usually don't publicize (on Web sites or other places) such benefits at all. This means that if you don't ask, you won't ever know if you could have taken advantage of this opportunity.

FREE FUN IS ALL AROUND YOU!

Where is it written that enjoying yourself involves spending money? Many people do not take advantage of the activities available to them every day, especially those that cost little to absolutely nothing. Sometimes we just do not realize that these options even exist. For some, we would often rather complain about having nothing to do (really our excuse for being lazy). Here are a few good examples of stuff to do that costs nothing or next to nothing. There is an endless amount of other options, and they stop where your imagination does.

Pack Up Your Stuff and Head to a Park

Public parks can be a great place to spend a cheap afternoon walking, cycling, inline skating, or just lounging under a tree looking for pictures in the clouds. Take a couple of friends and a Frisbee, and you'll be set for the afternoon. Before you head out, however, it is a good idea to ask your resident adviser or another student who has been around for awhile to find out if a park is safe.

CHEAP$KATE

Some colleges and universities have bicycles or hiking equipment you can borrow free of charge. Inquire at the student activities or athletic offices.

Bring Your Friends Together for a Card Game

Spades, Go Fish, Old Maid, Slap Jack, and even solitaire are all card games that are fun and entertaining. Even if you cannot find anyone who knows how to play one of these games, they are relatively easy to teach. Some students bring a deck of cards with them to school for something to do on a rainy day (or when they are broke). Even if you do not have a deck of your own, either the dormitory or the student commons often has a gaming area where you can sign a deck out with your student ID card. If you do not know how to play any of these games, you may want to learn a few before you get to college.

Unorthodox Card Games

Welcome to the world of action-card gaming. These days there are a number of somewhat unorthodox card games on the market, and you would be surprised how many college students play them. Magic: The Gathering, Pokémon, Dragon Ball Z, Duel Masters, and a number of other trading-card games are popular just about anywhere you go. The nice thing about these card games is that once you know how to play one of them, you have the ability to play just about all of them. The basic game plays out the same way, and it is just the terminology of the items that changes.

Attend Free Events

If you are bored, and you like to get all dressed up, but have nowhere to go (that you can afford), try attending campus or community-hosted activities. Even if you are not broke, you should attend some of these events—school administrators often determine the budget for student activities by looking at how many students attend these hosted events or participate in on-campus activities. So, if you want your school's student activities department to offer more or better stuff, then you should help them out by attending at least a few events a semester.

SAVVY STUDENTS SAVE

If you need something to do and don't want to spend money, there are always plenty of places where you can volunteer your time. Local YMCA or YWCA, Red Cross, day care centers, and retirement communities would be delighted to have the assistance. You would keep a hold on your money *and* do something good for your local community.

Community Events Can Be Cool

Outdoor festivals, flea markets, and other local events are fun and often charge no admission. Does the local community host an annual pig-calling festival? Do they have a fall pie-eating contest? Find out. Often enough, events such as these get posted in a section of the university newspaper or monthly student activities calendar (if your school has one). Don't be a stick in the mud. Expose yourself to a new community by attending events such as these—the stories that come out of them make for great ice-breakers when meeting new people!

Learning from and Laughing with Guest Lecturers

Each year, the administrators of colleges and universities spend a fortune trying to attract scholars, writers, thinkers, comedians, and sometimes even celebrities to giving lectures or seminars. However, fewer students are regularly taking advantage of this opportunity than did in former years. Sometimes, institutions do not actively promote these guest speaker lectures due to a limited amount of seating, which they fear might cause a problem with overcrowding.

However, most schools do have an available schedule of expected speakers with a description of their backgrounds, an announcement of when and where each lecture will be held, as well as what subject the speaker is covering. This is a great opportunity for college students. It can offer you a broad range of exposure to some very interesting and brilliant personalities in today's world—politicians, authors, columnists, and the experts in their fields of study are all examples of the types of people who are on the college lecture circuit each year. These days, for example, former president Bill Clinton is paid big money to speak at American universities, as are scholar authors such as Dr. Evans Lansing Smith, former Texas poet laureate James Hoggard and his wife, linguist Dr. Lynn Hoggard, as well as popular celebrities such as reality TV cast members and real-life heroes.

Students Get In Free!

Campus recreation or some other form of student activities department often hosts free on-campus (and sometimes even off-campus) events for students. All you need in order to get through the door at one of these activities is your student ID. Second-run (sometimes first-run) movies, intramural sports, hosted games, social events, poetry readings, ethno-cultural festivals, and a number of other events and activities are often made available to students every week throughout the academic year. Get out there, and get involved—for free!

Chapter 11

FIGURE OUT HOW TO MANAGE YOUR FUNDS

Money can be a lot like food—when you have enough to eat, it seems as though there is plenty of it, so do you ever find that you just eat as much you want? However, when your cupboards start to look bare days before your next scheduled shopping trip, you start to regret your previous overindulgence. Use money as you should use food—as you need to. Don't spend if the situation isn't a necessity, and always be sure to have some in reserve for when times get rough. Make sure there is at least as much money coming in each semester as there is going out. You don't want to run out of money before the end of the semester because you have blown your spending money on unnecessary stuff.

KEEP A BUDGET!

Budget, budget, budget. Keeping a budget can keep you out of trouble and can even allow you some "play" money if you stay on track! Learning to keep a budget is a good habit to get started on early. The reason a budget is so important is that it lets you know exactly how much money you have coming in and where certain portions of it will have to go. That means you can wonder, "Do I have enough money to go out dancing with my friends?" and be able to check your budget to find the answer.

Rule Number One—Follow the Budget

As with most other things in life, follow through is important. A budget that is written down but ignored is completely worthless. If you do not stick to your budget, it completely defeats the purpose of having one. Sticking to your budget will aid in preventing you from making the all-too-easy mistakes of overspending, "accidental splurging," or (heaven forbid) sending too much money for a bill, or (even worse) sending the wrong check for the wrong bill. All that fun and excitement you're having can come to a screeching halt when the $200 you were supposed to give to a roommate for rent "accidentally" got spent on a night out with some friends.

SAVVY STUDENTS SAVE

Here are some qualities of a good budget: accurate income projections, inclusion of expenses that don't happen every month (such as auto repair and income taxes), tracking and recording of spending, and a line item for savings. A good budget should also give you a meaningful picture of where your money goes and where you might be able to cut costs.

MR. CHEAP'S GUIDE TO PAYING FOR COLLEGE

Most people who manage money well have a monthly budget. Students are somewhat unique because they tend to have more "semester" expenses than monthly ones. One good budget method is to start your budget by determining your semester income.

Add up your projected job income for the semester (after taxes), along with your scholarships, grants, loan proceeds, and of course any cash expected from parents. Then calculate your educational and other fixed expenses. These are the ones you cannot cut. They include tuition, room, meal plan, books and required supplies, utilities (if you live off-campus), transportation expenses, and insurance. After identifying your income and fixed expenses, you should determine your variable expenses for the semester. These are the optional things you spend money on, as well as the expense items that vary from month to month. Some items in this category include cell phone and text messaging costs, gas or bus costs, eating out, clothing, entertainment, and other miscellaneous expenses. Do you have anything left over after you subtract your fixed and variable expenses from your income? If not, you are in deep water! What can you live without? There's got to be something!

Rule Number Two—There Are No "Accidents"

Nobody "accidentally" spends money. That would be physically impossible. The only thing even remotely close to accidentally spending money is having it stolen. The truth about these "accidental" situations is that the spender was not keeping tabs on the finances. You may say, "I thought I had more money in my account." Think what you like, but remember that the bank is going to charge overdraft fees regardless of what anyone thought.

If you find yourself feeling uncertain about how much money you have and whether it is okay to spend it, then you should pick from only one of two possible options. Let's break it down for you:

The first option . . . is to verify your balance by balancing your checkbook and checking your records against the bank's. Most banks offer account services over the phone or Internet, making it easy to know how much you've really spent. Be sure to take into account an estimation of any checks you have written lately that may not have cleared. Once you know how much is in your account, you can decide whether spending is a prudent choice.

The second option . . . is simple—you can just wait and come back when you know you have enough money (this is probably the best option, anyway).

There is no third choice. (If you think the third choice is to ignore the budget, you need to go back to rule number one.)

Rule Number Three—Never Break Rule Number One

The best way to keep a budget is in advance. When you receive a paycheck, go ahead and write out any and all expenses for that pay period. However, just because you have money left over does not mean you should feel free to go out and spend all of your surplus cash. Once you have accounted for your expenses, the best thing to do is to cut that amount in half. This remaining amount should be allotted for spending or what some people refer to as "walking around money," and the other half put into either a savings account or other investment plan (such as a Section 529 plan).

MR. CHEAP'S GUIDE TO PAYING FOR COLLEGE

The basics of budgeting are the same for students as they are for anybody else: list the sources of your income, such as savings from your summer jobs, financial support from your parents, financial aid from the school, scholarships, and income from your job (if you have one). Then list your expenses, such as tuition, books, groceries, gas, entertainment, and so on. Subtract your expenses from your income and be sure to get a positive number!

After you have followed a budget for a while, it may need to be updated by eliminating categories you no longer need or adding an additional expense. Stay as consistent as possible, but make adjustments when necessary. Use credit cards only in emergencies and pay off the balance as soon as possible. Use cash instead of credit cards whenever you can.

CONVENIENCE VERSUS FRUGALITY

Convenience is a funny thing, and it is often surprising how much people are willing to pay for it. For example, an express train ticket might cost $15 for an hour's journey. However, you could also take the local and make several connections for only $3 each, for a total trip of two hours. That's $9 the long way with a couple of inconvenient connections, and $15 for the short and easy way. Honestly, which one would you choose? Most of us would choose the express. Why? It is faster and more convenient. However, sometimes frugality means sacrificing convenience to save a little cash.

These days you may find yourself in a situation where the long, inconvenient way is the only way that you can afford to get to where you are going. But it doesn't have to be like that forever—so suck it up and take those extra couple of minutes to relax and enjoy the trip.

Bicycle Versus Car

No, "bicycle versus car" doesn't mean finding out who would win in a game of chicken. It just means that if you have a car, you might be tempted to drive from one place to another on campus. While that is a lot quicker and more comfortable than slinging the twenty-pound backpack over your shoulder and huffing and puffing up and down hills (not to mention dealing with inclement weather), it costs you money. If you think of the gas money you would save, in addition to the obvious health benefits of walking or riding a bicycle, you may want to let the car sit in your parking space until you really need to drive some distance. Better yet, just bring a bicycle and leave the car at home with your parents. Then you won't have to pay for gas or a parking permit.

CHEAP$KATE

Here's something simple you can do—use coupons. Coupons can save you a lot of money when you buy groceries and other necessities. In addition, restaurants often run specials and promotions that make it affordable to go out to dinner once in a while.

Cafeteria Versus Fast Food

Your school dining hall may not have the best food in the world, exactly, but if you have a meal ticket, or meal money, you should use it. Not using it is just as good as flushing money down the toilet. If the dining hall is open, and you have paid to be on the meal plan, then it is a waste of money to eat out. This does not mean you can never eat fast food or go out to a restaurant—just don't do it every night. Going out to eat all the time can be a very easy habit to fall into. To motivate yourself to stay on campus, try dividing the cost of your meal plan by the number of meals it covers. Thinking of each skipped meal in terms of actual dollars may help you realize what a waste of money it is.

SAVVY STUDENTS SAVE

Oftentimes money for food is part of the cost of tuition. If your meal money has already been allotted, don't waste it! Even if you're not hungry or you've already eaten, use your money to buy bottles of water or nonperishables or snacks from the food mart.

Super-Sizing Means Too Much Food and Money

Why just get the regular combo meal when you can super-size it? Come on, who among us really eats that many French fries or drinks that much soda (before it goes flat and gets watered down by melting ice)? Very few of us do. Super-sizing is something that fast food corporations thought up to get customers to spend an extra fifty cents or so on more fries and few extra ounces of soda, all of which adds up to about a cost of a few pennies for them.

The truth is, you are better off just getting the combo. If you're still hungry after that, order a little something extra. This will cost you less over time than just super-sizing all your meals because you think you are getting a better deal. You actually might be getting more for your money, but the extra fries you pay for will often end up being thrown in the garbage, along with that flat soda you could not bear to finish.

If your expenses are less than your income, you are in good shape as long as you stick to your spending plan. If your expenses are *more* than your income, you need to find ways to cut spending or increase your income.

CURB IMPULSE BUYING

One of the biggest threats to a student's finances can be the pitfall of impulse buying. If you don't know the term, it's exactly what it sounds like—the rampant spending of money with little or no regard for any kind of planned budget. These impulse spenders often spend money that they do not have, or they spend money faster than they can earn it. Either way, this is a really fast way to dig yourself into a deep financial hole. Develop some method to curb spending impulses—if not one of the suggestions given in this book, then something else, just as long as it works for you.

The Twenty-Four-Hour Rule

The twenty-four-hour rule is a good one to follow. Basically, it means that you start out by planning all of your purchases in advance. Then, if you see something that you'd like to buy but have not planned on buying (meaning it is not figured into your budget), then you have to wait a minimum of twenty-four hours before actually forking over any cash. You may wonder how this can do any good. Often when we first see something we want in the store, we are excited, enthusiastic, and acting on the adrenaline/endorphin rush we get from that impulse. Waiting a day to buy something gives that rush some time to wear off. Maybe after that much time, you will realize that it wasn't such a good deal after all. You may also find out there is something else you want even more that you couldn't have bought if you'd chosen to go with your impulse.

Leave Your Card at the Dorm

Being able to resist just whipping out that magic credit card every time you see something you want can be a lot easier than you might think. The most foolproof method for doing this also happens to be the easiest method—just leave the credit card in your dorm room! Walking around with a loaded credit card can be very dangerous. Keep yourself free and clear of trouble by leaving the plastic somewhere other than in your wallet (such as a strongbox, a locked drawer, or a safe).

The best thing about cash is that everybody accepts it! Of course, most businesses are set up for credit transactions because they are more common. However, sticking to cash is a good way to avoid spending more money than you actually have. Once all of your cash runs out, so does your ability to keep spending.

Don't be shy with relatives. Keep a running "wish list" to pass on to relatives. Nothing would make Grandma happier than to put together a basket of much-needed practical items for you. Gift cards and certificates are also great "wish list" items because they are so easy to buy and give.

BECOME A PENNY-PINCHING PRO!

Penny pinching is more than just an anal-retentive tendency—it is a way of life. For some reason penny-pinching got a bad connotation, but why? There is nothing wrong with being the kind of person who sees a pen on the ground and picks it up to see if it is still good. There is also nothing wrong with going through the pizza sample line at the grocery store a second time. Are you a cheapskate? If so, stand up and be proud of who and what you are! If not, consider the following pointers, and maybe you can become one, too!

Free Toiletries

There is no reason to let yourself become the Stinky Steve or Nasty Nancy of your dorm hall. Toiletries are always available; you just have to know where to look. If you are an athlete for your institution team, for instance, you will likely have a number of opportunities to stay in hotels. Some members of clubs and organizations also have opportunities to travel. Hey, those toiletries come with the cost of the room, so grab up all that you can—soap, toothpaste, shampoo, conditioner, and any other hygiene product you can find is free game. Just don't go crazy and start raiding the housekeeping cart in the hall. Taking what you paid for is one thing—flat-out stealing is wrong.

Dollar Stores—You Need It? They Got It!

Dollar stores are awesome! Yes, you do sometimes have to sacrifice a certain level of quality if you buy things there. However, it is always better to have a cheap version of a necessary item than not have it at all. If you want to pay a dollar for each item, then be sure that the store is actually a "dollar" store, not one of those stores where everything is just dirt cheap. For example, Dollar General is not a dollar store; it is a store where things are "generally" a dollar. The Dollar Tree, however, *is* a dollar store. Everything's a Dollar is also a dollar store, because, well, everything is actually a dollar. Of course, if you have no other options, Dollar General will do.

Thrift and Outlet Store Clothes

Don't worry—going to a thrift store these days does not necessarily mean being limited to shopping at the local Goodwill. In fact, outlet malls as well as clothing stores such as Ross, TJ Maxx, or Marshalls have made bargain hunting for brand names somewhat of a hobby for the American shopper. Paying a fair price for nice items is no longer a practice restricted to the extremely poor.

Clothing is something you need, but you don't necessarily *need* brand names. While some students like the crisp, preppy look of expensive and fashionable designer label clothing, there are plenty of other students who are completely comfortable with the idea of purchasing certain items at secondhand or discount stores. Not only does this idea appeal to those who are frugal at heart, it also gives students an opportunity to express themselves through one-of-a-kind creations that cannot be found in today's trendy stores or high-dollar fashion catalogs. Of course, this may or may not be your cup of tea, but for many money-wise students, the idea of getting their clothes at a fraction of the cost is very appealing.

CHOOSING AN ALTERNATIVE SPRING BREAK

Spring break is a time to party for many college students. Money is the last thing on many students' minds as they head in the direction of sunny beaches and a week of nothing but good times! But why come back to debt? Take care not to fall into the trap of blowing all of your hard-earned cash (or worse yet, make the mistake of charging your trip on a credit card) for a luxury experience that you know you cannot afford. Why not investigate alternative, more cost-efficient spring break trips? Many colleges now offer these trips as a part of their service work programs.

For example, you might sign up to volunteer with a group such as Habitat for Humanity. Habitat for Humanity even lets you travel for free, just as long as you commit a certain number of service/volunteering/work hours while you are at your chosen destination. This is an option that could involve some hard work, which may not sound as appealing as a care-free week of soaking up some rays on the beach, but you will be able to save a ton of cash and end your spring vacation with the feeling of satisfaction in knowing you have helped those less fortunate than yourself. And Habitat for Humanity trips might take you to a part of the country that you've never seen before—it's still traveling, if not a vacation!

Each college or university will have its own program requirements and budgets for these kinds of programs, so the number of hours required and travel expense compensation will vary from school to school. However, if you enjoy service work, this could be a great opportunity.

WHAT ABOUT *COMPLETELY FREE* COLLEGE COURSES?

If your high school has a college access program where you can attend a local college or take college credit courses after school free of charge, you are sitting on a gold mine! You may even be able to get double the benefit for your effort— high school *and* college credit. Jump on any opportunity you have to take Advanced Placement, International Baccalaureat, or dual enrollment courses. Even if you have to pay for these courses while you are in high school, they are a significantly lower cost than if you took the same course in a traditional college setting—plus they will look good on your resume and college admissions application.

BUDGETING PAYS OFF—NOW AND LATER

Even people with ridiculously high incomes can (and do!) run into financial difficulty by spending more than whatever their income is. It is amazing what we spend money on that we don't really need. Truly good money managers learn to spend within their financial boundaries early and stay within them throughout their lives. If you create a budget and manage your finances well when you are a student, you are likely to be good at managing money later (when you have a lot more of it).

Chapter 12

CONTROL YOURSELF WITH CREDIT CARDS

There is a very small (if not non-existent) gray area when it comes to credit cards. Nine times out of ten, credit cards are either your saving grace or your worst nightmare. They can help you out when you need it the most or they could kick you out when you're on your last legs. If you learn how to be responsible with your cards, you can make it work . . . but you need to know what you're doing! This section is meant to help you identify the good, the bad, and the ugly sides of the credit card world.

DON'T FALL INTO THE TRAPS

Everyone has received one of those letters marked "Important Credit Information Inside," or something to that effect. When you open it up, what's inside? That's right, a "preapproved" credit card, with "magic" credit. Be warned—there's no such thing as magic when it comes to the world of money and money lending! Cards like this are mailed out by the hundreds of thousands each year to first-year college students. These students have no credit, and therefore do not have "bad" credit. However, credit card companies believe that seventeen- to nineteen-year-old students have little to no concept of how money works. As a result, young (and inexperienced) costumers can get themselves into some serious financial trouble with cards such as these, where all they have to do is dial a number, answer a few questions, and shazam! They have a shiny new card that will buy them anything up to the credit limit.

Credit Is Not a License to Spend!

Having a credit card does not mean you have a green light to immediately max it out. With every purchase you make, you should think, "where will I get the money to pay for this" at the end of the month. If you have to think about it for more than a minute, put that item down and walk away before it's too late! Credit cards were designed to give you a little extra spending power when you *need* it! This does not include using the card to buy things that you cannot afford or to live a frivolous lifestyle that is far beyond your means. A good rule for using credit is to use it when you *have* to. For example, when the car you use to get to work and school breaks down, you can use the card to pay for the repairs that you cannot afford at the moment. (Just to clarify, sometimes a running car is a necessity; a completely new wardrobe is not.)

CHEAP$KATE

Using credit cards is not always a bad decision. They may offer very low rates—sometimes even zero percent for a period of time, with no annual fee. However, paying off this debt before the interest starts to accrue or increase is absolutely essential.

Good Credit Can Be Sweet As Honey

Less stress, lower interest rates, and favorable background checks for employment—these are some of the sweet benefits of having a good credit history. Credit bureaus compile your overall credit history and then when someone needs to know how well you manage credit, they go to a credit bureau and order a copy of your credit report. That report shows your debt, if you make your payments on time, and if you were ever late in making any loan payments. If you have a good report, you are more likely to be approved for a loan, get lower interest rates, or be hired for a job.

Bad Credit Sticks Longer Than Superglue

Seven years! That is how long it takes for a bad credit report to be wiped from your record! This means that foreclosures, surrenders, and repossessions of any kind will be there on your credit record for the entire world to see for no less than seven years. This can even have an effect on your ability to get a job, especially if you want to work in jewelry, management, or security occupations.

Why would bad credit keep a person out of a job? And why single out people in jobs having to do with jewelry, management, or security occupations? Well, for those jobs you almost always have to be bonded (a type of insurance that protects the employing company for losses in the case that you turn out to be a thief). For a bond, they do a credit report check, and if you have what they deem to be too much bad credit on your credit report, that bond can be next to impossible to get. No one wants to have someone with financial troubles handling too much cash or highly valued items. Sure, you are allowed to put your own comments/explanations on your credit record—but it probably won't do much good.

SAVVY STUDENTS SAVE

It can be a real pain, but you should always read the fine print. If you find something you do not understand or that concerns you, go to a professor, a lawyer, or a parent to have them explain it. Don't call the credit card company for an explanation—not unless you want them to give you a sugar-coated and misleading answer designed to get you to see things their way.

WHAT YOUR FICO SCORE MEANS TO YOU

The number that lenders get from a credit bureau that tells them how risky a borrower you are is called a FICO Score. A statistical model that uses your credit information from the past seven years determines your FICO Score. It looks primarily at your credit history, payment history, amount of loans outstanding, new credit, and types of credit. Education and car loans are better than credit card debt, which is another good reason to limit the use of credit cards.

Typically, creditors rank you as a good, average, or poor credit risk based on your 3-digit FICO number. The highest FICO Score is 900 and anything better than 680 generally qualifies you as a good risk. A score between 620 and 680 is considered average risk, and a poor credit risk is a score below about 620–650.

There are three credit bureaus that will send you a free credit history report upon request. Some financial advisers recommend that you request and review your credit report for accuracy annually. Paying your bills on time is critical to keeping your credit report favorable. Also, decrease existing levels of debt any time you can.

Stay Ahead of the Game

Request a free credit history report annually from the three credit bureaus: *www.equifax.com*, *www.transunion. com*, and *www.experian.com*. Review each report for accuracy and report any errors or discrepancies immediately!

RATES AND FEES—THE FACTS!

The annual percentage rate (referred to in most paperwork as the APR) can usually tell you how much interest you are going to pay on the balance of your credit card. However, keep in mind that this does not include fees and charges that are outside the category of interest. There may be so-called "hidden fees" that are kept from your attention with that low interest rate dangling there in front of your eyes. In addition to comparing the interest rates of different cards, watch for the ones that include these annual fees or other hidden costs.

Many cards offer low introductory APRs. Be sure you know how high the interest rate will rise after the introductory rate expires. Two cards that seem to offer the same terms may actually end up costing you quite different amounts in the long run. This is another perfect example of why reading the fine print on your credit card agreement is so important.

Credit card companies will often drastically raise their interest rates (sometimes to as much as 24 percent) after a customer makes a certain number of late payments. Read the fine print and know whether the payment is considered posted on its postmark date or on the date it reaches the bank or the credit card company. Unfortunately, once you accrue a few late payments, the credit card companies can start charging you the inflated interest rates for as long as you have the account. So before it gets to be too late, or even better, before you even *get* the card, look into these details! Knowing what you're doing can save you from debt and despair!

Variable Rates and More

A credit card company might choose to use a variable or a fixed rate to charge you interest. This can have a significant effect on what you end up paying just to use your card. Credit card companies using variable-rate plans base the fluctuation of rates on set indices. Often they will use the prime rate, one-month, three-month, or even the six-month treasury rate. If not, they will likely use the federal funds or federal reserve rate, also known as the "discount" rate. Most of this information can be found in the money or business sections of major newspapers.

Fixed Rate Plans

So, now you know there are variable rates, so are there ones that stay the same? Yes, these are called, you guessed it, fixed rates. Fixed-rate plans may be a couple of percentage points higher than a variable rate; however, you do get the advantage of knowing that your interest rate will not change without your knowledge. Variable rates are exactly what they say they are—variable. This means that they change, up or down. You take your chances with a plan like this.

If your rate is fixed, however, there is a piece of legislation called the Truth in Lending Act that requires the lender to provide no less than fifteen days' notice before increasing your interest rate. In certain states, laws require credit card companies to give you even more advanced notice. Some financial analysts argue that since a fixed rate can be increased after a fifteen-day notice, this plan is not all that dissimilar from a variable plan, which is subject to change at any time with no prior notice. The difference is that if you are notified of the change, you will potentially have the chance to switch to a new card before the changes take effect, if you so desire.

SAVVY STUDENTS SAVE

Identity theft is a common and understandable concern! Some credit card companies are now willing to offer you a protected guarantee in the case that you become another faceless victim of Internet fraud or identity theft. This kind of protection plan is referred to as an Internet fraud guarantee, and it is a good thing to take advantage of whenever it is made available.

When you are trying to choose between two credit card offers, look closely at both plans. If you decide to choose a variable-rate card, find out if there are caps on how high or low your interest rate can be. For example, if the lowest variable rate possible on one card is 17.5 percent, and rates are currently going down, choosing another option might not be such a bad idea.

Paying Dearly

No matter the plan you choose, accept the fact that you are going to be making monthly payments. And make those monthly payments! The more you put them off, the more trouble you will get into. If you find yourself in a bind, you can pay the minimum and that's better than nothing!

Each credit card company has its own way of determining your monthly minimum. Some companies start by calculating the interest rate. Once the interest rate is figured, the credit card issuer then adds a number of percentage points (the margin, as it is called) to this rate to come up with what the consumer will be charged.

Sometimes they choose to use a different formula to determine the rate charged. For this, they usually multiply the rate by a certain number that they refer to as the "multiple" (no one really knows how this number is decided on, save the ones who come up with it), or they add the rate to the margin and then multiply by the multiple. Confused? Don't worry. All you really need to know about the monthly payment is that you need to pay it, and that this is the *minimum* you should pay each month.

LIMITS EXIST FOR A REASON!

Getting yourself over a credit card's maximum limit is like digging yourself a ten-foot-deep hole. Instead of climbing out when you had the chance, you paid no attention to how deep it was getting and just kept right on digging while you were still in it.

You see, once you break a credit card's maximum credit limit, the fact that you are no longer able to use the card may be the least of your problems. At that point, the credit card company does one of two things. If you have been a good customer and always make your payments regularly and on time up until now, they might raise your limit. (This may be more convenient for you, but it is dangerous because it makes it extremely easy for you to get yourself into even more debt.)

CHEAP$KATE

Be sure to pay all your bills on time. If you live in an apartment, this includes your rent and utility bills. If you own a car, it could include your car or insurance installment. In addition to maxing out your plastic, late payments are another way to ruin your credit.

The second thing they might do is much worse (and kind of underhanded when you think about it). Some credit card companies penalize their customers with an over-the-limit fee, which is charged each month until the customer gets back under the limit. It can be as much as $20 (on top of the interest you are already paying).

Let's take a look at an example:

Suppose you are planning on paying your card's minimum, "low monthly payment" of $40 a month. You are $200 over your credit limit, with a balance of $2,200 at 10 percent interest—you can be in some serious trouble. From the $40 you decide to send in, the company first deducts the "over the limit" fee of $25, which leaves only $15 that goes toward your actual payment. If your interest is 10 percent on a balance of $200, then your interest alone is $22! You haven't even paid that off for the month, let alone started paying off your actual purchases!

If this is the way you pay your bills, your balance will not go down—in fact, it will go up! That leftover $15 from your payment will be deducted from your interest of $22, roughly leaving an unpaid amount of around $7. Well, guess what? Your balance is now $2207! That's right! You sent the credit card company the minimum $40 monthly payment, and you are now in rougher shape than you were when you started. Even worse—you are still over your limit, which means the same thing will happen next month. You are paying them regularly, but your balance just goes up and up.

CHEAP$KATE

According to the federal reserve, consumer debt hit $1.98 trillion in October 2003, up from the $1.5 trillion reported in 2000. (This figure includes credit card debt and car loans, but does not include mortgage debts.) This report showed that credit card debt alone was at $735 billion, with the average individual cardholder's outstanding balance at about $12,000. Kind of scary.

DIGGING OUT OF A HOLE

At this point you may be wondering how in the world you would ever be able to get yourself back under the limit once you've gone over it. If the balance continues to go up, how do they ever expect anyone to pay it off? The truth is that they don't want you to pay it off. They're happy as long as you just keep on sending monthly checks while they let your debt keep on rising.

Of course, the best thing for you to do is not use your card to make charges that you know will exceed its set limit. You should also never allow yourself to use credit cards as a way to live in a style beyond your financial means. Use your credit card as an alternative to cash when necessary (for example, reserving a hotel room often requires a credit card), not as a substitute for money you do not (and will likely never) have. If you stick to this basic philosophy, then you should have little to no trouble being able to pay off your monthly credit card balance.

CHEAP$KATE

Don't think that running up credit card debt will help you qualify for more financial aid. Consumer debt due to lifestyle choices is not taken into consideration when financial aid is determined.

However, if this advice comes a little too late for you, don't despair. There is a way to get your balance back down below your credit limit. Unfortunately, the hard truth is that once you reach this point, you are going to have to shell out some major cash to get things back under control.

Get It Over With

The first choice is to find a way to pull together enough to pay down your balance to a point well under the credit limit. In the example used earlier, this would mean the $207 that you're over your limit, plus another $25 to cover the next month's "over the limit" fee, and another $22 to cover interest charges.

In order to get yourself back under your maximum credit limit, you would have to make a single payment of $255.08. (That's an additional 25 percent on top of how much you went over your limit. See how those credit card companies get you?) If this is your method of choice, you're going to have to take a deep breath and just write the check.

A Bit at a Time

Your second choice is to cancel the card and pay off the balance a bit at a time. (Once you have canceled the card and charges have ceased, this can be as little or as much as you are able to pay each month.) If you do this, it is imperative that you do not get another card! Believe it or not, the credit company will try to get you to take another one once they have you back under the limit.

Minimum Payments Will Get You Nowhere!

The third choice is definitely the worst. In fact, it's not even an option but an example of what not to do. Just keep paying minimum monthly payments and let your balance continue to go up. This is not exactly among the wisest of decisions, but plenty of college students still opt for it.

Most cards, including Visa, Discover, and Master-Card make it very easy for you to follow this third path—be aware of this so you can avoid paying them forever. These cards offer what is known as revolving credit. This means they let you carry a balance, which they charge interest on (they call these finance charges). They will also require you to make a minimum payment. The minimum payment is commonly around 5 percent of your balance or $10, whichever is highest. Your payment varies depending upon your balance, the interest rate, and the method by which your finance charges are being calculated. As you learned above, if you only pay this minimum payment, your balance is more likely to continue to rise than to start going down.

BUILDING GOOD CREDIT WITH THE "RULE OF THREE"

The "Rule of Three" is a fairly foolproof and easy plan to follow. Basically, it governs the number of credit cards you can have. Your best bet is to start off with only one card. If you want to get a different card, with a higher balance, lower interest rate, or promotional offer, that's fine. However, if you insist on having multiple credit cards, never have more than three.

Start with One Card

The best thing to do, especially while you're in college and still learning about credit, is to limit yourself to one card. If you have a $1,500 balance on one credit card with a 7 percent interest rate, it will not be nearly as complicated to pay it off as the same total debt spread out over three different credit card companies—$500 on one card with a 10 percent interest rate, $500 on another card at 12 percent, and $500 on a third card charging 7 percent. The best way to start out is with only one card and then wait a year or two while you build up a good credit record.

Pay for Purchases Immediately

Later in life, there are going to be things that you will need and not be able to afford to pay in full. When this time comes, you do not want to have the credit mistakes of your past coming back to haunt you. (Remember that bad credit sticks around for seven years.) However, to start out on the right foot on your credit report, here is a tip—go ahead and get a credit card, but do not use it in the usual fashion.

SAVVY STUDENTS SAVE

If you have bad credit, and know that you have bad credit, be very wary of any guaranteed offers for credit approval. Operations such as these take advantage of those who cannot get credit elsewhere. Unfortunately, the price of approval is often an interest rate of over 20 percent.

Here is how it works. First you need to save up enough actual money to buy a relatively expensive item (such as an MP3 player or digital camera). Once you have that money in the bank, write out a check for that amount, paid to the order of the credit card company. Put the check in an envelope, address it to the credit card company, and make sure you have a stamp on it. Now go to the store and purchase the item on your credit card. As you are driving home, drop the envelope in the outgoing mail. By doing this, you will never have to worry about your balance getting out of control, and you will build strong credit.

Chapter 13

DON'T BE BLINDSIDED

Sorry to break this to you—but financial aid changes every year, as does the cost of tuition, room and board, and other expenses. So no matter how successful you have been at preparing yourself financially and finding ways to pay for college, you should brace yourself for the continued diligence it is going to take to renew existing financial aid each year and to find additional sources of assistance. Don't short-change yourself or your money! Stay on top of paperwork each year, and keep looking for ways to save, and you'll be fine!

A CONTINUAL SEARCH FOR DEALS

Many families make the easy mistake of thinking that everything that can be done regarding college financial aid must be completed early (things like all the paperwork, confirmation corrections, and other assorted details/red tape necessary to receive financial aid). It is true that early awareness and planning help keep you from missing opportunities, but do not forget that additional opportunities may pop up at any time. Be resourceful, and investigate every new circumstance as a potential new opportunity for acquiring additional financial aid.

SAVVY STUDENTS SAVE

You should always keep in mind that no matter what stage of the college process you are in now, you should be continuously researching to find out about the financial aid or scholarship/grant opportunities presently available. Scholarships and new financial aid programs are created all the time, but it is up to you to stay on top of them. How will you know what's new out there if you just stop looking?

Going Through "Major" Changes

Every new circumstance you encounter or new experience you become involved with has the opportunity to offer you hope by opening the doors to new financial aid possibilities. For example, if you for whatever reason decide to change your major (or minor), you may be able to apply for a scholarship now that was not available to you before. As a business administration major, liberal arts scholarships were not open to you. Let's just say that while you are taking a required English course, you suddenly discover that you absolutely love mythological studies. You decide right then and there to change over to a liberal arts major. Suddenly, those liberal arts scholarships that were out of your reach before are now wide open for you to start applying for.

The Door Swings Both Ways

Despite the fact that a new major can open up paths for new financial aid opportunities, remember that this is a door that swings both ways. Even though you may have gained scholarships and financial aid possibilities by picking a new major, you have also cut yourself off from those resources that were available only to students in your former major.

Along the same lines, if you started out in an associate degree program at a two-year institution, but you change your goals and decide to go to a four-year college or university, you may be eligible to receive new grants or scholarships. But there may be other kinds of aid for which you will no longer qualify.

DID YOU MISS A DEADLINE?

Is it already too late for you to make the deadline for this year? Has the "last minute" already lasted a minute? Has the opportunity for financial aid come and gone, leaving you coughing on the dust of its wake? Do not fear! Even though it may not make you feel any better right now, there is always another chance to reapply next year (or, sometimes, even next semester). Instead of beating yourself up over what a pickle you feel like you have gotten yourself in, start taking the initiative now to make the most of the situation.

The first thing you need to do is find out what deadlines you have already missed. Be sure to mark them down for next year so that you don't miss them again. Now remember that a year can be an awfully long time for you to hold onto (and keep track of) something, so be sure that you store a list of these dates in a place where they will not only be safe from destruction (doggy teeth, baby hands, and so on), but where they will not be forgotten between now and the time you need them. Also file any paperwork that you have already started so this will be handy when you're ready to officially restart the application process.

So You Missed the Boat

As you sit waiting for the next year to roll around, be sure you don't waste all that time sitting around, twiddling your thumbs and staring at the ceiling until you think you see faces in the spackle patterns. You could at least find a full-time job and start working on some extra savings to help pay for your tuition. However, if you're still set on getting started with your education, you do have a few remaining options. You might want to think about considering a deferment of your enrollment until the second (spring) semester, or perhaps you could postpone your enrollment until the following academic year. This will still allow you to go to your chosen school, and it may give you the financial aid you need to afford it.

SAVVY STUDENTS SAVE

Be sure to always make, file, and keep copies of any paperwork having to do with your financial aid. Applications, essays, letters of approval/award, and other important documents should all be duplicated.

MR. CHEAP'S GUIDE TO PAYING FOR COLLEGE

Consider Community College

Another last-minute option to consider is enrollment in a few core requirement courses at a low-cost institution such as the local community college. By doing this for a semester or two (or even three), you give yourself some transferable course credits, along with enough extra prep time to plan more for your academic future. You will also be able to avoid missing the boat when the next financial aid application deadlines roll around.

IMPORTANT TIPS TO STAY IN THE GAME

College is expensive. There are no if, ands, or buts about it. No matter who you are or what your financial situation is, you will have to drop a significant amount of cash on higher education if you choose to enroll. So how can you maximize the ways you pay and minimize payment? Remember that nobody else is responsible for finding that money and placing it in your lap. It is up to you to research your options, complete the forms, and do any follow-up work. Help is available through your high school guidance office, federal and state agencies, college financial aid offices, loan officers, and friends who have been through the process before, but students and parents themselves must work together and take the initiative. Every student's situation is unique, and the most qualified person to help you is you!

Never Dismiss an Opportunity

Finding money to pay for college is not something you should wait to do until a week before classes begin. You need to start early and keep searching throughout your college years for opportunities to obtain, earn, or save money. Do not look only for scholarships. Other kinds of aid are often just as good (and remember that some people use the terms scholarships and grants interchangeably). No- or low-interest loans can also help you pay for college.

A wise person once said, "It is okay to borrow money if it will help you make money later." If you apply yourself in college and pursue a career that you enjoy, the borrowed money will feel like a good investment once you have the job of your dreams. Work opportunities are another thing to consider while you are in college or between semesters. Besides helping you earn money for college, they can sharpen your job skills, provide valuable experience, and give you something to put on your resume.

CHEAP$KATE

Some types of aid are guaranteed, or automatically renewable, while others require you to apply again. Be sure to know which types of aid you receive require a renewal application. College could cost a lot more the next year if you give up thousands of dollars by not making that new application for certain types of aid after they have expired!

Don't Get Discouraged

You may find that you have exhausted all possible sources of aid, but don't give up! Budget an hour or two every week to continue to investigate your options. At some point, whether it's a week or a month later, you may discover a new scholarship opportunity. Also, as you progress in your major and advance in class level, other possibilities may become available. Free money is the best way to pay for college because you don't have to pay it back, but don't forget about ways to save or earn money. Not spending money unnecessarily, for example, is an effective way to free up money to pay for college.

An education is something no one can ever take away from you! Very few people who have graduated from college regret the sacrifices it took for them to acquire their education. It is a goal worth sticking to, and for most families, the joy of seeing their graduate accept a college diploma is one of life's greatest thrills. Just keep working hard, continue searching for ways to pay for college, and keep your eyes on the prize at the end. Your accomplishment will be even sweeter for knowing that you did not give up.

CHEAP$KATE

Stay focused. Money isn't everything, but when you graduate and enter the real world, with really big bills to pay, a college degree can pay off big. In addition to higher earnings potential, often there are differences in employee benefits by level of education (better retirement plan, more vacation time, better insurance plan, etc.).

Know All the Facts

It is a jungle out there, and it is easy to get lost in all the terminology and paperwork. But don't be intimidated! You can find out what you need to know if you invest some time and ask questions. Use the experts at your disposal, both in your high school and at the colleges you visit. Write down the important information. You may understand it at the time but find that you are confused later. Detailed notes will help you understand what you forms you need to complete and by what due dates.

When you decide on a college, remember that many people out there are willing to work with you to help you succeed. You are definitely not alone. Whatever questions you have, or difficulties you encounter, whether they are academic, social, or financial, people are ready to help. They will do as much as they can to answer your questions and to let you know your options. Think of your parents, admissions counselor, academic adviser, financial aid administrator, and other key people in your college experience as partners in your education. If you work together with them, you can find your unique pathway through your education and enjoy one of the most rewarding experiences possible.

BRACE YOURSELF FOR THE UNEXPECTED!

Always remember that no matter how prepared you think you are, you can't plan for everything. This is something that both parents and students should understand because unexpected circumstances can and likely will happen. Most of these unforeseen circumstances revolve around a single universal truth: Things change!

"What do you mean, things can change," you ask? Well, take a look at just some of the possibilities:

Majors—It is common for all students to change their major focus of study at least once, if not more often, during their college careers. Just because you choose a major in advance does not guarantee that this will be the degree you will graduate with.

Minors—These, too, are known to change.

Goals—Yes, they may be called "four-year" institutions, but that does not guarantee a degree in four years. Understand that a student's first and last year should have lower class loads than the middle two (or three) years.

Relationships—Break-ups happen (even if both parties left home for the same university). Pregnancies happen, boyfriends/girlfriends quit school and join the Navy, and so on.

These life events/choices could affect your college education, and parents, you should brace yourselves for them. As a parent, you also need to understand that if one or more of these occurrences takes place, what your student will need (more than anything) is your encouragement, love, and support. Try to keep the amount of chastising to a minimum, as too much lecturing about all the "should haves" and "could haves" (along with the occasional "why didn't you") might not only alienate you from your student but cause him or her to lose hope when he or she needs it the most. Be there for your children. They need you—whether they are willing to admit it or not.

Appendix A

FINANCIAL AID GLOSSARY

academic year: An institution's educational time period, consisting of one twelve-month year, the academic year usually begins in July and ends in June. The year is divided into standard academic terms of quarters, trimesters, or semesters. Each institution must designate whether its summer term is considered the beginning or the ending of the academic year.

accrual: The accumulation of interest, usually applied on a monthly basis. Some educational loans, such as the unsubsidized Stafford loan, allow for regular payment of accrued interest, so the loan balance remains at the principal amount until the student enters repayment.

adjusted gross income (AGI): This amount is calculated on a tax filer's federal income tax return. It is the taxpayer's income minus certain allowable amounts, such as student loan interest.

American College Testing Service (ACT): A nonprofit organization that does research and provides assessment testing for educational purposes.

amortization: A loan's repayment is scheduled over a specific period of time, during which the principal decreases, or amortizes. Payments include both principal and interest.

assets: Generally speaking, assets are owned items that can be converted into cash. When completing financial aid applications, be sure to understand which assets must be reported and which should not be included. For example, when completing the FAFSA, the value of a family's primary residence is not counted as a part of the parents' or student's total assets.

assistantship: This type of financial aid is usually provided for graduate students. It waives all or a portion of the student's educational expenses in exchange for teaching, assisting, or involvement in research/experimental work.

balloon payment: A large payment used to pay off 100 percent of the remaining balance of a loan. This is an option with certain educational loans.

base year: On financial aid forms, the tax year that is used to determine how financial aid will be made available and/or awarded. Usually refers to the calendar year prior to the one in which the student will attend college.

bursar: A treasurer or business officer at a college or university.

campus-based programs: Federal financial aid programs for students that are managed by the institution. The institution determines eligibility and distributes award amounts. Current campus-based programs include the Federal Supplemental Educational Opportunity Grant (FSEOG), federal work-study, and the federal Perkins loan program.

capitalization: A term for interest that accumulates on top of already unpaid interest. If a borrower pays off the interest on a loan as it is accrued, there is no capitalization.

CSS profile: A financial aid application created by the College Board, a national nonprofit association.

commuter student: A student who lives with one or both parents, or some other relatives, while attending college courses.

MR. CHEAP'S GUIDE TO PAYING FOR COLLEGE

consolidation loan: This type of loan combines two or more educational loans into one new one by paying off the original debts and creating one new, larger one in their place.

cost of attendance (COA): The estimate of a student's educational expenses for an academic period of time. The costs generally included in a student's cost of attendance are tuition, fees, room and board, books, transportation, and personal expenses. Institutions may also include additional items. A student's total financial aid package is not allowed to exceed his or her cost of attendance.

custodial parent: For financial aid purposes, the parent with whom the student lived with for the most time during the past year. If the student did not live with any one parent more than the other, then the parent who provided the highest amount of financial support is considered the custodial parent. If the custodial parent has remarried, then the new spouse is also required to provide financial information that will be included in the calculation.

default: Failure to repay a loan according to the legal agreement originally signed by the borrower. Default status appears on the borrower's credit report and can prevent further loans from being granted.

deferment: A legal postponement of an individual's obligation to pay back a loan. Many educational loans are automatically deferred until the time a student graduates from college or ceases to be enrolled as at least a half-time student.

delinquent: A debtor who has failed to make a loan payment by the required due date. Usually a late fee is assessed, and the borrower has a certain amount of time to make the required payment before the loan is considered to be in default.

demonstrated financial need: Usually the difference between the student's cost of attendance (COA) and the expected family contribution (determined through the FAFSA). A student's demonstrated financial need will not be the same at every college and university, mainly because the cost of attendance varies.

dependency status: Students are considered either dependent or independent in terms of their eligibility for financial aid. Status is determined based on a number of criteria, including age, number of dependents, and military service.

disbursement: Money paid out on behalf of the student. Financial aid is usually disbursed in equal parts over the course of the academic year (as in once a semester).

endowment: The property or funds that provide an institution of higher learning with a permanent source of income. Some colleges and universities have endowed scholarships, which are funded with the earnings or interest of a donor's monetary gift to the school.

entitlement program: This is a type of financial aid that guarantees all eligible students will receive the authorized amounts (because they are "entitled"). The Pell Grant program is one example of an entitlement program.

expected family contribution (EFC): The amount of money that the student and family are expected to pay toward the student's educational expenses over the next academic year. It is determined by a formula developed by Congress, called the federal methodology.

Federal Application for Student Aid (FAFSA): A financial aid application form provided by the U.S. Department of Education. It collects income and asset information of the student and student's parents (if the student is dependent). Most institutions require that students complete the FAFSA in order to be considered for financial aid.

Federal Family Education Loans (FFEL): The "umbrella" federal loan program that includes federal Stafford loans (whether subsidized or unsubsidized), federal PLUS loans, and federal consolidated loans. Borrowers of loans that fall under the FFEL are required to apply through private lenders, and the federal government guarantees the loans.

federal methodology: The mathematical formula, developed by Congress, used to calculate a student's expected family contribution (EFC).

federal Pell Grant: A grant entitlement program provided by the federal government for undergraduate students with financial need.

federal Perkins loan: A low-interest, campus-based loan program for both undergraduate and graduate students. Federal Perkins loans are subsidized, and the repayment interest rate is set at 5 percent.

Federal Parent Loan for Undergraduate Students (PLUS loan): A federal loan program specifically designed for the parents of college students. The PLUS loan program has a variable interest rate, which is capped at a maximum of 9 percent.

Federal Supplemental Education Opportunity Grant (FSEOG): A campus-based program provided for undergraduate students who have an exceptional amount of demonstrated financial need. Priority must be given to Pell Grant recipients who have the highest demonstrated financial need.

federal work-study: A campus-based program for undergraduate and graduate students who have a demonstrated financial need. It provides part-time employment with an hourly wage. Students are encouraged to work in jobs related to their specific academic program of study.

fellowship: A type of financial aid, usually awarded to college graduate students, that provides for an allowance or cash stipend for the purpose of funding a student's special focus of study.

financial aid officer (FAO): The administrator at a college or university who is primarily responsible for interpreting and implementing financial aid regulations, policies, and programs.

financial aid package: The combination of all the financial aid options available to the student for the academic year. Additional sources of financial aid may be incorporated into a student's financial aid package throughout the academic year.

forbearance: A temporary or complete discontinuance of the repayment of a loan (often by the borrower). Some educational loans have possible forbearance options if they occur under certain circumstances.

grace period: The time after a student graduates, or ceases to be enrolled in courses as at least a half-time student, before the student must begin to make repayment of a tuition loan.

grant: A type of gift aid that does not need to be repaid, usually awarded on the basis of need and sometimes on the basis of an applicant's skills, accomplishments, or some other qualifying criteria.

guaranty agency: The organization in each state that administers the FFEL (federal family education loans) program in that state.

institutional student information record (ISIR): An institution's version of the student aid report, or the response from the federal processor after a student has filed the FAFSA. Only institutions listed by the student on the FAFSA will receive an ISIR.

interest: The amount that accrues at a set percentage rate on the amount originally borrowed (the principal). The interest paid on a loan is the amount it costs to pay the loan back (that is, the amount it cost to borrow the money in the first place). Interest must be paid to the lender, along with the principal amount that was borrowed from the lender.

loan entrance and exit counseling: A requirement for some educational loans to inform the student of a loan borrower's rights and obligations. Institutions can provide this counseling by providing information sessions, one-on-one counseling, or through an online counseling program.

National Student Loan Data System (NSLDS): The database of borrower information for federal loans, including outstanding balances, status of loans, and disbursements made. The information comes from institutions, guaranty agencies, and the U.S. Department of Education.

outside scholarships: Scholarships that are provided from a source outside of the institution the student attends.

packaging: The determination a financial aid administrator makes concerning a student's financial aid eligibility for various types of aid. Packaging can be done through a computer program or manual calculations.

personal identification number (PIN): A unique identification number that serves as a student's or parent's electronic signature on the online FAFSA. A person's PIN can be used to access other federal financial aid information online and to electronically sign other documents.

promissory note: A legal document that lists the borrower's conditions and terms of a loan. It includes both principal and interest information, as well as provisions for deferment and cancellation.

satisfactory academic progress (SAP): An institution's standard of progress, which is required for continued participation in a number of educational programs. It must include a quantitative component and a qualitative component (that is, how many classes the student is taking and the grades being earned).

student aid report (SAR): A report that summarizes the student's data inputs as recorded on the FAFSA, lists the student's EFC, and may provide further information or instructions for the student.

subsidized loan: A federal student loan for which the U.S. government pays the interest while the student is enrolled in college courses as at least a half-time student.

tax credit: A dollar-for-dollar reduction in the amount of tax obligation that can be deducted directly from the amount of taxes the individual owes.

tax deduction: Expenses that can be subtracted from taxable income (as figured on state and federal tax returns), thus lowering the amount of tax owed.

tuition payment plans: A program that enables a family to make regular, periodic payments toward any of a student's educational expenses that are not covered by financial aid. This type of plan may be offered by the school or by a private lending institution.

unsubsidized Stafford loan: A federal student loan that accrues interest in the same way as any other type of loan.

verification: A process that compares the student's FAFSA information with the student's and the parent's tax return information as well as certain other submitted documents. Colleges and universities must verify students who have been selected by the CPS (central processing system).

verification worksheet: A form that families must complete for the financial aid verification process. This worksheet is provided by the institution and collects necessary information to be compared to a student's FAFSA as well as other verification materials.

W-2 form: A statement of the wages that an individual earned during the previous tax year. This form is required to complete all tax returns as well as the FAFSA.

Appendix B

FURTHER READING

A Is for Admission, by Michele A. Hernandez.

The Best 366 Colleges, 2008 Edition, by Princeton Review.

College Handbook 2008. Published by the College Board.

The College Board Scholarship Handbook 2008. Published by the College Board.

The College Board Index of Majors & Graduate Degrees 2004. Published by the College Board.

College Admissions Trade Secrets, by Andrew Allen.

Colleges That Change Lives: 40 Schools That Will Change the Way You Think About College, by Loren Pope.

The Fiske Guide to Getting into the Right College 2007, by Edward B. Fiske.

The Fiske Guide to Colleges 2008, by Edward B. Fiske.

Greenes' Guides to Educational Planning, by Howard Greene and Matthew W. Greene.

Paying for College: The Greene's Guide to Financing Higher Education, by Howard R. Greene and Matthew W. Greene.

Harvard Schmarvard, by Jay Mathews.

How to Go to College Almost for Free, by Ben Kaplan.

The Insider's Guide to the Colleges 2008: 34th Edition. Yale Daily News.

On Writing the College Application Essay, by Harry Bauld.

The Pocket Idiot's Guide to Surviving College, by Nathan Brown.

Scholarship Almanac 2005. Published by Peterson's Guides.

Colleges Unranked: Ending the College Admissions Frenzy, by Lloyd Thacker.

The Scholarship Scouting Report: An Insider's Guide to America's Best Scholarships, by Ben Kaplan.

The Unofficial, Unbiased Guide to the 331 Most Interesting Colleges, 2005, by Kaplan Staff.

Paying for College Without Going Broke 2007, by Princeton Review.

The Big Book of Colleges 2007, by College Prowler, Joey Rahimi, Kelly Carey, Megan Dowdell.

Appendix C

ONLINE RESOURCES

College Search Web Sites
www.studentaid.ed.gov
www.embark.com
www.collegenet.com
www.mapping-your-future.org
www.petersons.com
www.gocollege.com
www.fastweb.com
www.collegeview.com

Textbook Sources
www.amazon.com
www.half.com
www.textbookx.com
www.textbookhound.com
www.ecampus.com
www.addall.com
www.abebooks.com
www.collegeswapshop.com
www.cheapcollege.com

SAT/ACT Information and Tips
www.collegeboard.com
www.act.org
www.review.com
www.petersons.com
www.sat-secrets.com
www.number2.com
www.mcps.k12.md.us
www.powerprep.com
www.4tests.com
www.viatouch.com/learn/SAT.jsp
www.studyguidezone.com
www.studysphere.com

Planning for College
www.fafsa4caster.ed.gov
www.adventuresineducation.
org
www.review.com
www.collegeispossible.org
www.studentaid.ed.gov
www.fastweb.com
www.gocollege.com

www.collegeanswer.com
www.collegeplan.org
www.collegeplanning.org

College Comparisons

www.usnews.com
www.overview.com
www.earnmydegree.com
www.campusdirt.com
www.go4college.com
www.collegeview.com
www.collegequest.com

Military Service and Department of Veterans Affairs

www.military.com
www.va.gov
www.vetfriends.com
www.1800goguard.com
www.usmc.mil
www.goarmy.com
www.army.mil
www.aerhq.org
www.af.mil
www.airforce.com
www.navy.mil
www.asvabprogram.com

College Savings Information

www.collegesavings.org
www.collegesavings.com
www.upromise.com
www.babymint.com
www.moneycentral.msn.com
www.finaid.org
www.americanexpress.com
www.savingforcollege.com
www.nysaves.org
www.scholarshare.com

www.brightstartsavings.com
www.independent529plan.org
www.usfunds.com
www.microinvesting.com
www.agedwards.com
www.529s.com
www.cfnc.org

Budgets, Debt Management, and College Loan Repayment

www.finaid.org/calculators/
www.erieri.com
www.mapping-your-future.org
www.ccsintl.org
www.cc-bc.com
www.creditstaff.com
www.youcandealwithit.com
www.nfcc.org
www.center4debtmanagement.com
www.creditreport-net.com
www.cs-america.com
www.ammend.org
www.consumerdebtsolutions.net
www.consumercredit.com

Tax Credit Information

www.irs.gov/taxtopics/tc605.html

Selective Service Administration

www.sss.gov

Social Security Information

www.ssa.gov

Internal Revenue Service

www.irs.gov

MR. CHEAP'S GUIDE TO PAYING FOR COLLEGE

Corporation for National Service
www.cns.gov
www.americorps.org

National Collegiate Athletic Association
www.ncaa.org

National Junior College Athletic Association
www.njcaa.org

U.S. Department of Education
www.ed.gov/finaid.html
www.studentaid.ed.gov

FAFSA on the Web: Application and Information
www.fafsa.ed.gov